HISTORIC CONNECTICUT MUSIC VENUES

HISTORIC CONNECTICUT MUSIC VENUES

FROM THE COLISEUM TO THE SHABOO

TONY RENZONI

FOREWORD BY FELIX CAVALIERE

THE History PRESS

Published by The History Press
Charleston, SC
www.historypress.com

Copyright © 2022 by Anthony Renzoni
All rights reserved

First published 2022

ISBN 9781540251121

Library of Congress Control Number: 2021949180

Notice: The information in this book is true and complete to the best of our knowledge. It is offered without guarantee on the part of the author or The History Press. The author and The History Press disclaim all liability in connection with the use of this book.

All rights reserved. No part of this book may be reproduced or transmitted in any form whatsoever without prior written permission from the publisher except in the case of brief quotations embodied in critical articles and reviews.

Advance Praise

As the promoter of the concerts in many of the music venues in this book, I hope you enjoy living the special memories this book will give you.
—*Jim Koplik, Live Nation president,*
Connecticut and Upstate New York

Tony Renzoni has captured the soul and spirit of decades of the Connecticut live music scene, from the wild and wooly perspective of the music venues that housed it. A great read!
—*Christine Ohlman, the "Beehive Queen,"*
recording artist/songwriter

Another skillful tribute to music and entertainment by Tony Renzoni. This time, Tony digs deeper into many of the great Connecticut music venues and artists, well known and local. When coupled with his earlier book Connecticut Rock 'n' Roll: A History, *we are shown a venue/artist montage that allows the reader the feel of having been there. Which I was and it does. I highly recommend this book!*
—*Ken Evans,*
of the Fifth Estate band

As a native son, it was always a pleasure to perform here in Connecticut. The music venues mentioned in Tony Renzoni's book bring back so many great times and memories. I had the good fortune of performing at many music venues throughout Connecticut, along with many talented artists.

At the New Haven Arena, I performed with two of my groups on the same show—the Five Satins and the New Yorkers. Also appearing that night were the Nutmegs from New Haven.

At both the New Haven Paramount Theatre and the Hartford State Theatre, I had the wonderful opportunity of appearing with my dear friend Roger Koob and his group the Premiers. I also met some of my favorite entertainers here in Connecticut—artists such as Wynonie Harris and The Clovers.

I wish to thank Tony Renzoni for renewing these wonderful memories in his book Connecticut Music Venues: From the Coliseum to Shaboo. *I highly recommend this book to music lovers everywhere.*
—*Fred Parris,*
of the Five Satins and the Scarlets

Looking back over the years, I am so proud to be one of the pioneers of the Connecticut music scene, along with great visionaries like Jim Koplik. And I am extremely grateful to the many fans and artists who have kept the "Shaboo Spirit" alive. There is nothing like the excitement of live concerts. For the many concert-goers throughout the U.S., I highly recommend this book!

—*David "Lefty" Foster, former owner of the Shaboo Inn and member of the Shaboo All-Stars*

Tony Renzoni reminds us of watching local music shows on television, when we were too young to go to concerts, and then finally, when we could drive, parking in the snow and walking into a warm venue to be amazed by the theatrics of Alice Cooper. I was reminded of sitting on the grass in an outdoor venue, as a young adult, watching Meat Loaf sweat through all seven songs from his Bat Out of Hell *album, and more recently, feeling the nighttime breeze while enjoying great songs from Felix Cavaliere's Rascals. The places, photos and stories entertain us throughout this wonderful new volume in Tony's Connecticut music book series.*

—*Warren Kurtz, contributing editor,* Goldmine, *the music collector's magazine*

Connecticut had its own great rock scene. Most of the musicians that played in the many Connecticut venues also played in New York City, so that kept the quality pretty high for bands.

The Flying Tigers played in quite a few Connecticut clubs and we had a very loyal fan base. At our concerts, our fans were well-acquainted with both our original Flying Tigers songs as well as the songs we played from the other band I am associated with—the Alice Cooper group.

Some of the clubs were quite rowdy and we have lots of memories to smile about. If you were there, you know what I'm talking about.

If you wish you had been there, all you have to do is read Tony's book.

—*Dennis Dunaway, Hall of Fame artist and cofounder of the Alice Cooper group, the Flying Tigers and Blue Coupe*

This book is dedicated to all the music venues that many of us have had the fortunate opportunity to attend as we watched our favorite artists perform live in concert. Whether or not these music venues still exist, they will always live on in our hearts and memories.

CONTENTS

Foreword, by Felix Cavaliere 11
Acknowledgements 13
Introduction 15

1. Music Venues—Past 17
2. Music Venues—Present 91
3. *Connecticut Bandstand*: TV Dance Show 129
4. *The Brad Davis Show*: TV Dance Program 143
5. The Gathering of the Vibes Festival 148

Appendix A. Interviews with Two Hall of Fame Legends 153
Appendix B. The Amazing and Mysterious Saga of
    the Mega-Hit Song "(Na Hey Hey) Kiss Him Goodbye"
    Recorded by a Bridgeport Trio 161
Appendix C. Behind-the-Scenes Photos of Artists
    (Including Some Rare Photos) 167
Bibliography 179
Index 181
About the Author 189

FOREWORD

Soon after "Good Lovin'" reached No. 1 on Billboard, the Young Rascals performed to a sell-out crowd at the New Haven Arena on May 7, 1966. Playing the New Haven Arena in those days was an exciting and enjoyable experience. The fan reaction there and all across the United States to "Good Lovin'" and our subsequent records was incredible. I have always been told that people not only enjoyed listening to our records but also loved seeing the Rascals live in concert. You see, that's the beauty of music venues and why they are such an integral part of the music process. Music venues serve as a place where the musician's music comes to life. When we put out a new single, we would debut it with the audiences in music venues throughout the country. We could tell our new record would be a hit by watching the fan reaction and feeling the energy in those concert venues. Performing live was such an important and fun part of the music business—and it still is for me! Without music venues, fans would be deprived of hearing and seeing their favorite band performing live in concert, which would be so unfortunate.

Whether it was with the Young Rascals, the Rascals or my solo career, Connecticut has certainly been an important part of my life. I have found that there was always a tremendous appreciation of music in Connecticut. The people there really support the arts. And it was a Connecticut native (Lori Burton) who helped launch our Top 100 singles debut, cowriting our first song, "I Ain't Gonna Eat Out My Heart Anymore," and also "Baby Let's Wait." Both songs appeared on our first album, *The Young Rascals*.

Foreword

The state of Connecticut has always had great venues to play, and we performed in the state many times. I have enjoyed playing in some wonderful small and large music venues in Connecticut, including the Mohegan Sun, the Yale Bowl, the Oakdale Theatre, the Shaboo Inn, Staples High School and the Ridgefield Playhouse and in concert with Ringo Starr and his All-Starr band. And I have enjoyed performing with very talented artists from Connecticut such as my dear friend Ronnie Spector, Big Al Anderson and the late great Laura Nyro.

I have always felt indebted to the fans in the tristate area of Connecticut, New York and New Jersey. That tristate area put us on the map and kept us on the map.

I have often been asked why I moved from New York to Connecticut. I grew up in Westchester, right across the border of Connecticut. I always looked over there at that beautiful green place and said *man that would be a nice place to live*. So I moved to Fairfield County and lived in Danbury for seventeen years. I recall driving to Bridgeport all the time and jamming with some very talented musicians there. And, of course, I recorded a number of songs with the Rascals and as a soloist while living in Connecticut. Connecticut was an ideal place to live in those days because it was located close to large markets such as New York, Massachusetts and New Jersey.

These days, I have been living and recording in Nashville, Tennessee. I have an active tour schedule planned with my band Felix Cavaliere's Rascals. I am so pleased to continue to play the Connecticut scene, performing at the brand-new Hartford Healthcare Amphitheatre and the Ridgefield Playhouse. Other Connecticut music venues are being planned.

I would like to thank Tony Renzoni for giving me the opportunity to write the foreword to his wonderful book. I highly recommend *Connecticut Music Venues: From the Coliseum to Shaboo* to music lovers everywhere!

—Felix Cavaliere

Hall of Famer Felix Cavaliere in concert. *Courtesy of Warren Kurtz.*

ACKNOWLEDGEMENTS

Colleen Renzoni, Dr. Kerry Renzoni, Sir Bronn, Felix Cavaliere, Al Anderson, Fred and Emma Parris, Jim Koplik, Phillip Solomonson, Larry Rifkin, Ivor Levene, Len DeLessio, Fred Fisher, David "Lefty" Foster, Bruce John, Kathy Barbino Mosgrove, Charles Rosenay, Marty Ganter, Cheri Miller Weymann, Burton Stahl, Ray Lamitola, Dorothy Yutenkas, Ginny Arnell, Marty Morra, Karen and Dan Mancinone, Russ Pettinicchi, Bill and Elise DeMayo, Bill Rienzi, Bill Koob, Dick Robinson, Art DeNicholas, Barbara Lyon, Charlene Massey, Charles Amann, Cynthia Lyon, David Miller, Deep Banana Blackout (Fuzz), Henry McNulty, Dennis D'Amato, Dick Sandhaus, Ellen Sandhaus, Mary and Joe Blacker, Lou Rizzuti, Jackie Cipriano, Joe Sia, Julia Fleischmann, Susan and Stephen Roche, Gary Shea, James R. Anderson, Jane Bouley, Jason Bischoff-Wurstle, Jeff Cannata, Jeff Potter, Jim Bozzi, Joe Suraci, Judith Fisher Freed, Larry DeLucia, Linda Sunderland, Lisa Reisman, Marilyn Hewitt, Mary Beth Welsh, Mary Stone, Nick Balzano, Nora Kaszuba, Paul Rosano, Peter Neri, Brian Dench, Randy L. Schmidt, the Reducers, Rose Marie DeGennaro DeMatteo, Tom Kaszuba, Stan Nimiroski, Brianna Kurtz, Tom Horan, Scott Spray, Andrea Spray, Wayne Gamache, Weaver Santaniello, Paula Renzoni Crean, Al Ferrante, Jayson Cutler and Steve Parker.

Thank you Christine Ohlman and Dennis Dunaway for all your advice and support. And a special thank-you to Warren Kurtz and Ken Evans for your invaluable assistance with this book. Finally, I wish to thank my book publisher (Arcadia Publishing/The History Press) and, of course, editors Abigail Fleming and Mike Kinsella for all their wonderful guidance and support during this entire book process.

INTRODUCTION

Any music scene, anywhere in the world, rises and falls on the music venues that nurture it. Historically, Connecticut's scene has had it all—from wonderful tiny dives to the grandest opera houses and coliseums, and everything in between: late-night blues clubs, iconic rock 'n' roll rooms, theaters of every size, outdoor stages and tents, Elks and Grange halls and fabulous festival grounds. Music lives here!!!
—Christine Ohlman

I remember the first live concert that I attended. I can still feel the anticipation, excitement and energy that was in the air throughout the music theater. And I still remember the fan reaction as the band played the first few notes of their opening song, the joyful cheering throughout the concert, the standing ovations and the request for encores. I still have that same feeling today as I make plans to attend concerts at my favorite music venues.

Throughout the years, music venues in Connecticut have played an integral part in the music scene of this state. Like many other states, Connecticut has had its fair share of popular and historic music venues. These venues ranged from large arenas such as the New Haven Coliseum and the Yale Bowl, which held many thousands of fans, to smaller venues such as legendary clubs like the Shaboo Inn and Toad's Place.

Connecticut music venues have hosted iconic artists of many different genres. Frank Sinatra performed at the New Haven Coliseum on several

Introduction

occasions. After his concerts at the Coliseum, Sinatra would make a point of dining at New Haven's famed Sally's Pizza restaurant, where they pulled out the red carpet for "ol' Blue Eyes." Sinatra also performed in other Connecticut music venues, including the Hartford Civic Center, the New Haven Arena and Foxwoods. The "King," Elvis Presley, wowed the audience when he performed at the Hartford Civic Center and the New Haven Coliseum.

Some of the performances that took place in these music venues are legendary. Take, for instance, the arrest of Jim Morrison (of the Doors) as he performed on stage at the New Haven Arena (the first ever arrest of a musician on stage) and the impromptu concert by the Rolling Stones at Toad's Place.

And I would be remiss if I didn't mention that many record stores served as host venues for local bands. Two very popular Connecticut music shops were New Haven's Cutler's Records and Waterbury's Brass City Records. Jayson Cutler, former owner of Cutler's Records, recalled: "Cutler's was not just a record store, it was a mecca for live performances by local bands who would introduce their music to fans in the New Haven area. Those were fun times for me."

Connecticut was also the home of two very popular television teenage dance programs: *Connecticut Bandstand* and *The Brad Davis Show*.

The purpose of this book is to give readers an insight into the music scene in Connecticut throughout the years. The book pays tribute to all the great Connecticut music venues, past and present, that have provided such unique experiences and wonderful memories for all of us who have had the opportunity to experience the excitement of live music concerts. The book also pays tribute to many of the very talented artists who have performed at these music venues. The performers mentioned in this book run the gamut from the very famous to those who achieved fame on a regional or local level. But, hey, it's all rock 'n' roll, regardless of the level of fame of these artists! And many of these performers, regardless of their level of fame, have had a very loyal fan base. All of the accomplishments by these musicians, both great and small, have shaped Connecticut's music culture. I am happy to report that Connecticut music is alive and well and continues to rock!

So, whether or not you are familiar with Connecticut's music scene, I think you will agree that nothing quite matches the excitement you will experience by attending a live concert in your state and at your favorite music venue.

This is a follow-up to my book *Connecticut Rock 'n' Roll: A History* and the second in my Connecticut music book series.

1
MUSIC VENUES—PAST

In the old days, we didn't have internet, Facebook, Instagram or any other social media—but we did have our music. And it was music that bonded us together. To me, the fans that attended the music venues that the Rascals performed in had that "community spirit." It was a community based on the fans' love of the music we played.
—Felix Cavaliere

New Haven Arena

In 1961, famed promoter "Wild Man" Steve produced a big show at the New Haven Arena starring Brook Benton, the Shirelles, Dave "Baby" Cortez and Little Anthony and the Imperials. The show also featured a Battle of the Bands contest featuring Connecticut bands: the Five Satins, the Nutmegs and Roger Koob and the Premiers.

The show was sold out, and each act received a great reaction from fans. When we were introduced, the Premiers received a thunderous ovation. Our fan club was out in full force. With Roger Koob's powerful lead voice and with the dance routines Joey Vece put together with splits and all, the group was all juiced up and the audience responded in kind. There was a lot of Connecticut pride on the line for that concert. And there was some serious talent in that room when you think of Fred Parris (Five Satins), Leroy Griffen (Nutmegs) and Roger Koob (Premiers). New Haven (and Connecticut) had a lot to be proud of that night.
—Bill Koob, of the Premiers

Historic Connecticut Music Venues

New Haven Arena. *Courtesy of the New Haven Museum.*

The original New Haven Arena on Grove Street in New Haven, Connecticut, opened in 1914 but burned down in 1924. The arena was reconstructed in 1927. As a music venue, the New Haven Arena hosted numerous iconic rock 'n' roll (and non-rock) concerts.

The New Haven Arena was an extremely popular venue for many years, attracting millions of fans (far beyond the Connecticut border) during its existence.

Elton John gave the final performance at the New Haven Arena on September 29, 1972, during his Honky Chateau tour. At the end of the concert, Elton threw out thousands of candy bars to an appreciative audience.

In 1974, the New Haven Arena was demolished. After the New Haven Arena was torn down, major concerts were held in the newly constructed New Haven Coliseum.

The following are some of the artists who performed at the New Haven Arena:

From the Coliseum to the Shaboo

Jim Morrison's Arrest on Stage at the New Haven Arena

One of the most famous (or infamous) events in rock history occurred at the New Haven Arena on December 9, 1967. On that date, Jim Morrison was arrested on stage during a performance with the Doors. He was charged with obscenity and breach of peace but was released early the following day. It is believed to be the first time that a rock star was arrested on stage during a performance. The incident was immortalized in the 1970 song "Peace Frog" by the Doors, especially the line "Blood in the streets in the town of New Haven." The opening act for the Doors on December 9, 1967, was the West Haven group Tommy and the Rivieras.

Top: Jim Morrison's mug shot, New Haven Police Department. Morrison was arrested on December 9, 1967, but was booked by the New Haven Police Department on December 10, 1967. *Public domain.*

Bottom: John Densmore of the Doors. *Copyright Ivor Levene.*

The Rolling Stones Scheduled 1964 Concert at the New Haven Arena

The Rolling Stones scheduled appearance at the New Haven Arena (canceled due to lack of ticket sales). *Author's collection.*

The Rolling Stones, billed as "England's Newest Sensation," were scheduled to perform at the New Haven Arena on June 18, 1964. Famed NYC WINS disc jockey Murray the K was to be the concert emcee. However, the show was canceled—due to lack of ticket sales! By the way, the ticket prices for this concert were two, three and four dollars. The Stones did appear at the New Haven Arena the following year (November 4, 1965).

Cream

Above: Ginger Baker of Cream. *Copyright Ivor Levene.*

Right: Cream performed at the New Haven Arena on October 11, 1968. *Courtesy of Dick Sandhaus.*

Sly and the Family Stone

Sly and the Family Stone played at the New Haven Arena on September 27, 1971.

The Young Rascals (Rascals)

The week after "Good Lovin'" reached No. 1 nationally, the Young Rascals performed at the New Haven Arena on May 7, 1966. The opening acts were the Connecticut bands the Shags and the Symbolix. The Young Rascals also performed in concert in 1967 at Westport's Staples High School. The opening act was the band the Loved Ones. The Young Rascals soon changed their name to the Rascals.

In the 1960s, the Rascals charted in the Top 40 thirteen times, including three No. 1 singles: "Good Lovin'" "Groovin'" and "People Got to Be Free." The quartet was composed of Felix Cavaliere on vocals and organ, Eddie Brigati on vocals and percussion, Dino Danelli on drums and Gene Cornish on vocals and guitar.

Top: Sly Stone. *Courtesy of Henry McNulty.*

Bottom: Young Rascals band members (*left to right*: Eddie Brigati, Felix Cavaliere and Dino Danelli) backstage after a concert at Westport's Staples High School, February 19, 1967. *Copyright Ellen Sandhaus.*

The Rascals were inducted into the Rock 'n' Roll Hall of Fame in 1997.

The Symbolix

> We had been together for about eleven weeks when we won the Battle of the Bands at Turkey Hill Road School. First prize was to open for the Young Rascals at the New Haven Arena. We were still the Symbolix at that time. For this occasion, we purchased English flag shirts at the Ice Cream Parlor in Westport.

Historic Connecticut Music Venues

> *We changed our name to Bridge about the time of the release of our song "It's a Beautiful Day." I wanted to name the band Osric after the gravedigger in Hamlet, but I was outnumbered. We did name our record label Kirzo, so it was a small victory there.*
> —Dennis D'Amato, of Symbolix and Bridge

The Symbolix band performed at the New Haven Arena, where they (and the Shags) were the opening acts for the Young Rascals. The Symbolix band was later renamed Bridge. Members of the band were Paul Tortora, Dennis D'Amato, John Mariano, Charlie Claude and Leon D'Amato.

New Haven Coliseum

> *Shape clay into a vessel; it is the space within it that makes it useful.*
> —Laozi

> *Likewise with a music venue it is how the space is approached rather than the building structure that allows for the magic of performance to take hold for both the artist and the audience.*
>
> *Many stages are hallowed ground where artists once defined their careers. Take, for instance, The Troubadour, CBGB, Checkerboard Lounge, The Fillmore and The Stone Pony. Some music venues are majestic architectural cathedrals with fine acoustics, such as Red Rocks, Carnegie Hall, the Hollywood Bowl and Grand Ole Opry. Other venues create intimate gatherings where performers make eye contact, become conversational and open up on stage (e.g., The Ark and City Winery). Connecticut has had its own historic venues (such as the New Haven Coliseum and Yale Bowl) that fans can harken back on where they saw their favorite artists and bands.*
>
> *Music venues are a significant part of the providence and magic.*
> —Phillip Solomonson, Philamonjaro Studio,
> performance/concert photographer, Chicago

New Haven Veterans Memorial Coliseum (better known as the New Haven Coliseum) was built to replace the New Haven Arena, which was demolished in 1974. Construction for the Coliseum was completed in 1972. The Coliseum held an estimated twelve thousand fans. For thirty-five years, the Coliseum was a major attraction for many national and

From the Coliseum to the Shaboo

The New Haven Coliseum. *Courtesy of the New Haven Museum Photo Archives.*

local artists and bands. The New Haven Coliseum met its fate when it was demolished at 8:00 a.m. on January 20, 2007. The Coliseum's implosion caused quite a commotion for the places and people in the nearby vicinity of the large structure. Over twenty thousand people gathered to witness the implosion.

The following are some of the artists that performed at the New Haven Coliseum:

Elvis Presley, "The King"

I saw Elvis Presley in concert at the New Haven Coliseum. I wasn't quite sure what to expect since it had been many years since he burst onto the music scene in 1956. The sold-out concert was outstanding, and the audience reaction was amazing. Elvis proved once again why he is the "King of Rock 'n' Roll"!

—Bill DeMayo

Elvis Presley performed at the New Haven Coliseum on July 16, 1975 (for two shows), and on July 30, 1976. Elvis has been inducted into numerous Halls of Fame and has received countless awards for his music achievements—too many to list. Elvis has been a major influence on many giants in the music industry, including the Beatles. In 1986, Elvis was one of the first inductees into the Rock 'n' Roll Hall of Fame. According to the Hall of Fame website, "Elvis Presley is, quite simply, the King of Rock 'n' Roll."

The Alice Cooper Band

> *I was an Alice Cooper fanatic since age fourteen. I remember seeing them in concert in 1972. I threw a pumpkin on stage, and Alice immediately smashed the pumpkin with his sword. I also saw Alice Cooper at the New Haven Coliseum during the band's glamorous Billion Dollar Babies tour a year later.*
>
> —Weaver Santaniello

The Alice Cooper band (originally called the Spiders) was one of the first rock acts to play the New Haven Coliseum when they performed there on Wednesday, December 26, 1973.

The Alice Cooper group members were Vince Furnier (stage name Alice Cooper), Dennis Dunaway (bass), Michael Bruce (rhythm, keyboards), Neal Smith (drums) and the late Glen Buxton (lead guitar). Furnier legally changed his name to Alice Cooper and has had a very successful solo career under

Alice Cooper band. *Copyright Philamonjaro.*

that name. The original members of the band joined Alice for a live tour of the United Kingdom in 2017. The band is famous for their elaborate, theatrical shock-rock stage performances.

In 2011, the original Alice Cooper band was inducted into the Rock 'n' Roll Hall of Fame.

Dennis Dunaway (Cofounder of Alice Cooper)

Connecticut's Dennis Dunaway was inducted into the Rock 'n' Roll Hall of Fame in 2011 as a founding member of the Alice Cooper band. Dennis also won a Grammy for cowriting "School's Out." The original Alice Cooper group sold millions of singles and albums and was on the cover of *Forbes* for having the largest grossing tour in 1973, over Led Zeppelin and the Rolling Stones. The *Billion Dollar Babies* album (recorded in Greenwich, Connecticut) reached No. 1 in America and Britain, and the group is recognized as the innovators of theatrical rock shows, which included giant balloons, hangings, snakes and spidery eye makeup. The group's movies are *Diary of a Mad Housewife*, *Good to See You Again: Alice Cooper* and *Super Duper Alice Cooper*.

Some of the clubs that Dennis and his bands performed in were far from subdued venues. Dennis recalled one such Connecticut music venue:

> *The Night Owl in Norwalk was another favorite music venue. It was a rowdy place. The popular drink was a Snake Bite, which was a shot of Yukon Jack and Lime Cordial. The Snake Bites flowed freely on stage*

Dennis Dunaway. *Copyright Philamonjaro.*

and in the crowd. One night, a fight broke out and two guys came crashing through the dressing room door. We had a stagehand named Eric that we called the Master of Disaster because whenever fights broke out, he would set off smoke bombs and empty the place.

Dennis currently records and tours with Blue Coupe, featuring Joe and Albert Bouchard of Blue Öyster Cult fame along with singers Tish and Snooky of Manic Panic. The Blue Coupe has performed in a number of Connecticut music venues, including The Warehouse in Fairfield. On November 12, 2019, Blue Coupe released their outstanding CD *Eleven Even*. Dennis performed at the New Haven Coliseum in 1973 with the Alice Cooper band.

The original Alice Cooper group recorded three songs on Alice's *Welcome 2 My Nightmare* album, re-recorded "School's Out" with Joe Perry and Johnny Depp for the *Hollywood Vampires* album, recorded two songs on Alice's *Paranormal* album and contributed two songs on *Alice's Detroit Stories* album with producer Bob Ezrin, which was released on February 26, 2021. They also joined Alice for a live tour of the United Kingdom in 2017.

The Who

Hall of Fame band the Who turned in a dramatic show at the New Haven Coliseum on December 15, 1979.

Left: The Who in concert. *Copyright Ivor Levene.*

Right: Roger Daltry of the Who. *Copyright Philamonjaro.*

From the Coliseum to the Shaboo

Gwen Stefani (No Doubt)

The popular group No Doubt performed at the New Haven Coliseum on April 12, 1996. No Doubt also played at The Meadows Music Theatre and Mohegan Sun. As a solo performer, No Doubt's Gwen Stefani performed twice at the Mohegan Sun.

U2

The rock band U2 played at the New Haven Coliseum on two occasions. The band performed at many other Connecticut music venues, including the Hartford Civic Center (nine times), Toad's Place, Mohegan Sun and Woolsey Hall. U2 was inducted into the Rock 'n' Roll Hall of Fame in 2005.

Bono (U2). *Copyright Philamonjaro.*

Tom Petty

Tom Petty and the Heartbreakers played at the New Haven Coliseum on four occasions. They also performed at the Hartford Civic Center (four times), Meadows Music Theatre (six times), Pinecrest Country Club and Lake Compounce. Tom Petty and the Heartbreakers were inducted into the Rock 'n' Roll Hall of Fame in 2002.

Tom Petty. *Copyright Philamonjaro.*

Gary Shea (of New England and Alcatrazz)

One of my favorite moments of playing arenas was at the New Haven Coliseum in 1981. On the bill were Foghat, New England and the Joe Perry Project. I stood there and marveled that all three bass players who

would shake the place that evening all grew up in Connecticut. I just thought that was really cool and I wish I had taken photos. It was a one-time thing.
—*Gary Shea, of New England and Alcatrazz*

Gary Shea was born and raised in Southington, Connecticut, and graduated from Southington High School. Throughout his career, Gary has been known for his melodic, straight ahead bass style. His focus has always been to play what the song calls for.

Gary switched from the guitar to the bass at the age of fifteen with his band the Insane. As Gary said, "I realized that the bass was the thunder behind the music and what you shake your body to. From that time on I fell in love with the low end and set out to shake everywhere I played."

Gary is currently a member of the rock band New England, which was formed by Shea, John Fannon, Jimmy Waldo and Hirsh Gardner. New England's songs have hit the Top 30, and the band has recorded three albums with producers Mike Stone and Todd Rundgren.

New England band. *Courtesy of Gary Shea.*

Shea is also a member of the heavy metal super group Alcatrazz. Shea, Graham Bonnet and Jimmy Waldo form the nucleus of the band. Alcatrazz has earned gold records and is known internationally for their musicianship.

Gary recalls an incident that he and his band Alcatrazz had at a club in New Haven:

> *Alcatrazz and Ted Nugent played the Twilight Zone in New Haven the summer of '84. It was hot, pouring rain and muggy. We blew the power during our first song. After two hours, the house was back with power. Ted decided we would go on with both our bands playing full shows. The bar was closed, and we finished at 3:00 a.m. The crowd was great that night.*

In Connecticut, the band New England performed at the New Haven Coliseum on July 31, 1981. Years later, Shea's band Alcatrazz performed at the Mohegan Sun. Reflecting on his career, Gary Shea observed, "If there is anything else in my career I would hope to achieve it would be to influence others to pick up an instrument and say, 'that's what I want to do.'"

THE HARTFORD STATE THEATRE

> *On April 17, 1960, the Premiers took part in a huge Easter Sunday show at the Hartford State Theatre. We shared the stage with such great artists as Johnny Nash, Frankie Lymon, the Cadillacs, Baby Cortez and comedian Red Foxx. I remember I was backstage in the dressing room playing on a set of bongos. All of a sudden, this guy stopped by the dressing room and asked, "Hey man, do you mind if I play those bongos"? I instantly recognized the man as Frankie Lymon. As a fifteen-year-old kid, I was awestruck! I never forgot that moment.*
>
> —*Bill Koob, of the Premiers*

The State Theater in Hartford was built in 1926. The theatre held four thousand customers, and at the time, it was considered perhaps the biggest movie theater in New England. It was known for its long outside marquee.

The theater drew the biggest names in movies, radio (Frank Sinatra, Perry Como, Doris Day) and big bands (Glenn Miller, Tommy Dorsey, Benny Goodman).

The State Theatre also hosted legendary performances by such iconic rock 'n' roll stars as Chuck Berry, Little Richard, the Five Satins, Buddy Holly and the Crickets, Frankie Lymon, the Nutmegs and the legendary Alan Freed concerts. It also played host to groups that were popular on a regional basis such as the Premiers.

Fans from Connecticut, Massachusetts, Rhode Island and New York (and sometimes farther) flocked to see their favorite stars and groups perform at the theater before it closed in 1962.

The following are some of the artists who performed at the Hartford State Theatre:

The Five Satins (and the Scarlets)

On December 3, 1960, the Premiers took part in another huge show featuring Dion, the Five Satins, Gary U.S. Bonds, the Passions, the Mello Kings, a young Gene Pitney and other great artists. Our group shared a dressing room with the Five Satins, which was a very fun experience. The Five Satins were an outstanding group and a fan-favorite wherever they performed!

As part of our performance, we wore these bright red neckerchiefs loosely tied around our necks. At one point we went to the edge of the stage, ripped off the red neckerchiefs and tossed them to the crowd. The fans went nuts. Our fan club was there in large numbers, and they were screaming their heads off. It was pretty late when we left the show. As we got outside, a group of girls, who were camped out, started to chase us. We ran down to George Street and then to New Haven's WNHC building where our cars were parked. What a crazy night!

—*Bill Koob of the Premiers*

In the 1960s, St. Mary's church basement served as a music venue for many high school students in the New Haven area. Every week we would make a point of meeting our friends there, listen to local bands and dance to the hit records of the time. The night always concluded with "the last four," a series of slow, romantic songs. Of course, a highlight of the evening was the beautiful song "In the Still of the Night" by New Haven's Fred Parris and the Five Satins.

—*Susan and Stephen Roche*

Considered one of Connecticut's most well-known and successful vocal groups, the Five Satins were formed by singer-songwriter Fred Parris in New Haven. Fred and the Five Satins achieved worldwide fame with their classic doo-wop tune "In the Still of the Night." This multimillion seller is the only song ever to have charted on the Billboard Hot 100 three separate times (1956, 1960, 1961) by the same artist, with the same version each time.

While Fred Parris was serving in the military, West Haven's Bill Baker took over lead vocals on the Five Satins' beautiful ballad and Top 10 hit "To the Aisle." The song also charted well outside the United States (for example, No. 5 on Toronto's CHUM radio). Baker passed away in Yale New Haven Hospital on August 10, 1994. He is buried in All Saints Cemetery in North Haven, Connecticut.

Before forming the Five Satins, Fred Parris was the lead singer and songwriter of a 1950s group known as the Scarlets. The Scarlets were an R&B/doo-wop vocal group from New Haven. Fred Parris and the other group members were still students at Hillhouse High School when the Scarlets formed in 1953. "Dear One," written by Parris, became a local hit for the Scarlets in 1953. After the Scarlets disbanded, Fred Parris formed the legendary Five Satins in 1955.

The Five Satins shared the stage with other Connecticut artists, such as the Nutmegs, the Premiers and Debbie and the Darnels. Over the years, the Five Satins have performed in a variety of music venues in Connecticut, including the New Haven Arena, Hartford's State Theatre, Paramount Theatre, Bridgeport's Kennedy Center and Actors Colony. The Five Satins were inducted into the Vocal Group Hall of Fame in 2003.

Fred Parris

I have such fond memories of performing in music venues in my home state of Connecticut and throughout the United States, Canada, and Europe. Sharing the stage with such great artists as Lloyd Price, Anthony and the Imperials and the Dubs (to name just a few) has been a beautiful experience for me. Forty years ago, the Satins performed in concert with Fats Domino at Atlantic City's Tropicana, and the casino did over $1 million per night while our show ran. My group, the Satins, were even invited to the White House where we were presented a special certificate of appreciation and a set of White House cufflinks. I also was pleased

> to be the first R&B artist featured in the Smithsonian Magazine in which I shared the story of my song "In the Still of the Night." Such wonderful memories!
>
> —Fred Parris

Fred Parris is an iconic figure and a much-loved individual in Connecticut. He has lived in Hamden (a suburb of New Haven) for many years.

During the 1950s, Parris formed the doo-wop groups known as the Scarlets and the Five Satins. In 1965, Parris formed another group, called Fred Parris and the Restless Hearts. Their recording of "Bring It Home to Daddy" in 1966 reached No. 1 on local charts in Connecticut.

Parris also recorded several songs with the soul/funk group Black Satin (1975 and 1976). The songs were written by Parris, produced by New Haven's Marty Kugell and arranged by Bridgeport's Paul Leka. The recordings took place in Leka's Connecticut Recording Studios on Main Street in Bridgeport.

On April 23, 2015, Congresswoman Rosa DeLauro introduced into the Congressional Record a tribute to Fred Parris on the House floor. The tribute states, in part, "One night, while on guard duty at 4:00 a.m., Fred penned 'In the Still of the Night,' bringing a musical gift to the world. Fred Parris is a true community treasure."

On February 22, 2016, a tribute to Fred Parris and the Five Satins was held at St. Bernadette Church in New Haven. Fred Parris and his lovely wife, Emma, were in attendance. Also in attendance was Vinny Mazzetta, the man who played saxophone on "In the Still of the Night." Mazzetta was instrumental in convincing then pastor of St. Bernadette's Church Father Charles Hewett to agree to let the Five Satins record songs in the basement of St. Bernadette's. The program was a celebration of the sixtieth anniversary of the iconic song "In the Still of the Night" by the Five Satins.

Fred Parris. *Copyright Peter Hvizdak and the* New Haven Register.

Incidentally, "In the Still of the Night" by the Five Satins played a prominent role in Martin Scorsese's *The Irishman* (2019), in which the song is played on three separate occasions in the movie.

Alan Freed

> *I hope you'll take my hand as we stroll together down our musical Memory Lane. The Big Beat in American Music was here a hundred years ago—it will be here a thousand years after we are all gone. SO— LET'S ROCK 'N' ROLL!*
>
> —*Alan Freed, "Mr. Rock 'n' Roll"*

One of the most popular and influential pioneers in the history of rock 'n' roll, Alan Freed gained legions of fans as a disc jockey, concert promoter, record hop emcee, TV host and film star. While at Cleveland's radio station WJW, Freed coined the phrase "rock 'n' roll." His fame grew while he was at WINS and WABC radio stations in New York City, when he earned the nickname "Mr. Rock 'n' Roll."

Freed described his rock 'n' roll music (which he called the big beat) in this way: "Rock 'n' roll is a river of music that has absorbed many

Alan Freed hosting the legendary Record Rendezvous R&B concert while at WJW (1951). *Courtesy of Judith Fisher Freed (estate of Alan Freed).*

streams: rhythm and blues, jazz, rag time, cowboy songs, folk songs. All have contributed to the big beat."

For years, Freed resided in Stamford, Connecticut, at his mansion known as the Greycliff Manor, which overlooked Long Island Sound. There, he hosted many music executives and made plans to bring rock 'n' roll to the big screen.

Alan Freed made a number of stage appearances, including popular concerts in Connecticut at Stamford's Plaza Theatre (December 7, 1956) and Hartford's State Theatre (March 6, 1960).

At one point, Freed was asked what he thought about rock 'n' roll . His response was this: "Let's face it. Rock 'n' roll is bigger than all of us."

Alan Freed was one of the first inductees into the Rock 'n' Roll Hall of Fame in 1986. In fact, Cleveland was chosen as the home of the Rock 'n' Roll Hall of Fame as a tribute to Freed.

Alan Freed died on January 20, 1965.

Chuck Berry

Chuck Berry was the first musician to be inducted into the Rock 'n' Roll Hall of Fame when it opened in 1986. As noted on the Rock 'n' Roll Hall of Fame website, Chuck Berry was inducted by the Rolling Stones' Keith Richards, who stated, "It's very difficult for me to talk about Chuck Berry 'cause I've lifted every lick he ever played. This is the gentleman who started it all!"

Known as the "Father of Rock 'n' Roll," Berry was a singer/songwriter/guitarist and a true pioneer of rock 'n' roll. Also noted in the Rock 'n' Roll Hall of Fame website, "After Elvis Presley, only Chuck Berry had more influence on the formation and development of rock 'n' roll."

Left: Chuck Berry with Alan Freed; *middle*: Buddy Holly; *right*: Little Richard and Bill Haley. *All images courtesy of Judith Fisher Freed (estate of Alan Freed).*

The lyrics to Chuck Berry's songs focused on teenage life. Who can forget Berry's famous duckwalk on stage, which he made famous in 1956? Chuck Berry was a major influence on subsequent rock 'n' roll musicians such as the Rolling Stones.

Berry performed at numerous Connecticut music venues, including Hartford's State Theatre (November 16, 1957 and March 30, 1958), Stamford's Plaza Theatre (December 7, 1956), the Bushnell Memorial (twice), the New Haven Arena (twice), the Hartford Civic Center and the Levitt Pavilion (with Little Richard).

Chuck Berry died on Saturday, March 18, 2017.

Buddy Holly

Legendary singer/songwriter/guitarist Buddy Holly (born Charles Hardin Holley) was one of the first inductees into the Rock 'n' Roll Hall of Fame in 1986. As noted on the Rock 'n' Roll Hall of Fame website, "Rock 'n' roll as we know it wouldn't exist without Buddy Holly." Buddy Holly was a true pioneer of rock 'n' roll, and he influenced a great many musicians, including Paul McCartney and John Lennon.

Buddy Holly and the Crickets performed at Hartford's State Theatre on November 16, 1957, and March 30, 1958. On February 3, 1959, Buddy Holly perished in an airplane crash along with Ritchie Valens and the Big Bopper, J.P. Richardson. This event was immortalized in Don McLean's song "American Pie" as "The day the music died."

Little Richard

Rock 'n' roll pioneer Little Richard (born Richard Wayne Penniman) performed in numerous concerts in Connecticut, including Hartford's State Theatre (February 26–27, 1956), the New Haven Coliseum, Toad's Place, Foxwoods Theatre, the New Haven Green (June 27, 1998) and Oakdale Theatre.

Little Richard was one of the first inductees in the Rock 'n' Roll Hall of Fame inaugural class of 1986. He was also inducted into the Songwriters Hall of Fame. Little Richard died on May 9, 2020.

Historic Connecticut Music Venues

Roger Koob and the Premiers

In December 1957, singer/songwriter Roger Koob started a doo-wop group with his brother Billy, their cousins Barbara Klump and Vin Klump and a close friend, Tim Vaill. This lineup was short-lived, as Barbara, Vin and Tim left to pursue other interests.

The groups that Roger Koob assembled had several personnel changes, and the names changed from the Premiers to the Travelers and the Frontiers at one point. The name change from the Premiers to the Travelers was made out of necessity. Unaware that the Premiers' name registration had lapsed, Roger was notified that a West Coast group had assumed the name Premiers. Roger was then forced to change the group name to Roger Koob and the Travelers. While the groups that Roger Koob formed had changed their names several times, locally they were always referred to as Roger Koob and the Premiers (or simply the Premiers).

The most successful group lineup was in the 1960–61 period and consisted of Roger Koob , Billy Koob, Joey Vece and Jonny Roddi. This is the group that recorded the popular songs "She Gives Me Fever" and "Daddy's

The Premiers. *Courtesy of Bill Koob.*

Little Girl." At the time, the members—Roger (twenty-one years old), Billy (sixteen), Joey (fifteen) and Jonny (seventeen)—were very young. Roger Koob was a great lead singer, Joey Vece had a talent for choreography and the group harmony was as tight as it could be. They were hitting on all cylinders.

Roger Koob's groups had a large, devoted fan club that followed their favorite group throughout Connecticut. In the mid-1960s, Koob also teamed up with New Haven's Bill Baker to form the singing groups David and Goliath and also the Buddies. Koob and the groups he assembled were popular in Connecticut, and their songs ranked high on local radio charts. They were also popular throughout the East Coast and even in Canada.

In 1973, Roger formed another group he called the Mudd Family and enlisted his brother Billy and their longtime friend Skip Voss. Roger then hooked up with Paul Stookey and Peter Yarrow (of Peter, Paul and Mary fame) to perform at a charitable event to raise money for a New Haven Jewish home for children. The event took place in New Haven's Bowen Field. The list of performers for this event was impressive, including such stars as Gordon Lightfoot, Mitch Rider and the Detroit Wheels, John Denver and the Staple Singers. Interestingly, the huge stage and scaffolding set up for this event were the same used for the famed Woodstock concert.

The Premiers performed at a number of music venues and record hops throughout Connecticut, including Hartford's State Theatre, Paramount Theatre, the Actors Colony, the New Haven Arena, West Haven's Quigley Stadium, Lake Compounce Record Hops, *Connecticut Bandstand* and *The Brad Davis TV Show*.

The Nutmegs

In 1974, the Premiers took part in an oldies tour of a number of Connecticut locations. The last stop on the tour was the House of Zodiac in West Haven. The lineup for this tour consisted of the Nutmegs, the Premiers and the Academics. The Nutmegs were the closing act and treated the fans to their nationally charted hits "Story Untold" and "The Ship of Love." The Nutmegs were one of the best a cappella groups of the doo wop era. They did some "killer" a cappella on this tour.

—*Bill Koob, of the Premiers*

The Nutmegs hailed from New Haven. The members named their group after the State of Connecticut's nickname—the Nutmeg State.

The Nutmegs had a major hit record in 1955 with their song "Story Untold." The tune peaked at No. 2 on the R&B charts and has become a doo-wop classic. Their other hit record was 1955's "Ship of Love" (No. 13 on the R&B charts). Also, "My Story" and "Whispering Sorrows" were local favorites in Connecticut and other U.S. markets ("My Story" was a Top 30 hit on Michigan's WKAR).

The Nutmegs performed at Hartford's State Theatre as part of the *Rhythm & Blues Revue* on November 20, 1955. They were also a featured group at the Alan Freed First Anniversary show in 1957 at the Brooklyn Paramount. The Nutmegs were known for their amazing a cappella sound, led by singer/songwriter Leroy Griffin.

THE BUSHNELL MEMORIAL (1960s, 1970s)

In 1967, I had the good fortune of touring with the great Gene Pitney as a member of the band the Fifth Estate. The tour was called the Gene Pitney Show. On the same bill as Gene were the Fifth Estate, the Music Explosion, the Happenings, the Buckinghams and the EasyBeats. At the time, all the bands mentioned were at the top of their games. The tour took us to many venues throughout the United States. We kicked off the tour in August 1967 at the Bushnell Memorial in Hartford.

I have fond memories of Gene and all the other guys we performed with. Gene had that incredible voice and was famous for delivering those dramatic, piercing climactic endings to his songs. By the time Gene took the stage, all the other performers would be backstage. So, during each performance, some of us would engage in a bet on whether or not Gene would hit the incredible high note on his hit song "I'm Gonna Be Strong." Betting against Gene would almost certainly mean losing money. Another somewhat insignificant but fond and funny memory for us is recalling how Gene would always play cards on the bus in his red polka-dot underwear. Gene was an extremely talented man yet a fun, down-to-earth guy.

—*Ken Evans, of the Fifth Estate*

The Bushnell Memorial in Hartford was built in 1930. The Bushnell hosted many iconic and well-known rock 'n' roll artists and bands such as Chuck Berry, Jerry Lee Lewis, Bob Dylan, Janis Joplin, Billy Joel, Bob Marley and the Wailers and the Beach Boys.

From the Coliseum to the Shaboo

Bushnell Memorial. *Author's collection.*

This venue was renamed the Bushnell Center for the Performing Arts and continues to thrive, featuring many cultural events and the celebrations of classical music with orchestras such as the Hartford Symphony Orchestra.

Other notable artists that performed at the Bushnell Memorial:

Jimi Hendrix

Jimi Hendrix performed at the Bushnell on March 22, 1968, and August 24, 1968.

Left: Bushnell ad for Hendrix's concert. *Courtesy of Dick Sandhaus*; *right*: Jimi Hendrix and the Experience, relaxing backstage at the Bushnell Memorial, 1968. *Courtesy of Henry McNulty.*

Historic Connecticut Music Venues

The Ronettes

The Ronettes performed in a number of Connecticut music venues, including the Bushnell Memorial (November 10, 1963), Yale University and Hartford's State Armory. The trio consisted of lead singer Ronnie Spector, her older sister Estelle Bennett and their cousin Nedra Talley.

The Ronettes were nominated for a number of awards and inducted into the Grammy Hall of Fame (1999) and the Vocal Group Hall of Fame (2004). After being eligible for a quite a long period of time (some would say too long), the Ronettes finally were inducted into the Rock 'n' Roll Hall of Fame on March 12, 2007.

Gene Pitney, the "Rockville Rocket"

> *I sang in church and school and always had a love for music, but it wasn't until the mid-fifties, when the first rock 'n' roll came roaring out of the radio, that it really got inside my head and wouldn't let go.*
>
> —Gene Pitney

The pride of Connecticut, singer-songwriter Gene Pitney, the "Rockville Rocket," was born in Hartford and raised in Rockville, Connecticut. While attending Rockville High School, Pitney formed a group called Gene and the Genials. In 1959, Pitney recorded four demo songs with a Hartford doo-wop group known as the Embers. The same year, he recorded a song under the name Billy Bryan. "Cradle of My Arms" by Billy Bryan (Pitney) was written by Winfield Scott, writer of the hits "Tweedlee Dee," "Many Tears Ago" and "Return to Sender." The song charted on several radio station surveys, including Syracuse's WNDR.

Pitney was also part of the duo Jamie and Jane. Jane was actually New Haven's Ginny Arnell. The duo recorded several songs that charted locally and in other parts of the United States. Ginny recalled: "It was fun working with Gene. He never went anywhere without his guitar. He was always thinking about new songs to write. He was a very slim, aggressive, handsome and talented young man who was going to achieve success at any cost."

Bill Koob, of Roger Koob and the Premiers, recalled an interesting conversation his group had with Gene Pitney:

From the Coliseum to the Shaboo

In 1959, our group the Premiers were performing at a record hop at Derby High School. I was singing lead on Dion's "Teenager in Love" when I noticed a couple leaning against the back wall of the gym. They looked like performers so when our performance was over I asked the DJ who they were. It turned out that the couple was Gene Pitney and Ginny Arnell. At the time, they recorded as a duo known as Jamie and Jane and collaborated on a song "Faithful Our Love."

A few years later, Gene Pitney was with record producer Marty Kugell in his Ansonia home. It was in Marty's basement where they worked on the presentation tape for Aron Schroeder that really launched Gene's career.

One night after Gene's rehearsal, Marty brought Gene to one of our rehearsals for a friendly visit. While there my brother Roger asked "Hey Gene, ya got any material for us?." Gene responded "I have a song, 'She's A Rebel,' that I am offering to a group. If they don't take it maybe we can work something out." The group turned out to be the Crystals, and they changed the title to "He's a Rebel" and into one gigantic hit. I'm not saying it would have been a hit if we recorded it, but it makes for an interesting thought.

Gene Pitney's music legacy is impressive. As a recording artist, Pitney had sixteen Top 40 hits, four in the Top 10. In the United Kingdom, he had twenty-two Top 40 hits and eleven Top 10 hits. His recording of "Something's Gotten Hold of My Heart" (a duet with Marc Almond) was a No. 1 hit in the United Kingdom and several other European countries. An international sensation, Pitney recorded complete albums in Italian and Spanish.

In Connecticut, Gene's recordings consistently charted well on the state's radio station music surveys. For example, Pitney was well represented in Hartford's WDRC Best Selling Sixty of 1961 music survey with his own recordings at No. 44 and No. 50, plus his penned "Hello Mary Lou" at No. 2 on this same 1961 survey. Also, "It Hurts to Be in Love" charted No. 5 on WWCO's 1964 survey.

As a songwriter, Pitney wrote hit songs such as "He's a Rebel" (No. 1 song for the

Gene Pitney proudly showing his Gold Record for his No. 1 UK hit "Something's Gotten Hold of My Heart." *Courtesy of Brian Dench.*

Crystals) and "Hello Mary Lou" (No. 9 hit for Ricky Nelson), and cowrote "Rubber Ball" (No. 6 for Bobby Vee in the United States and internationally No. 4 in the United Kingdom and No. 1 in Australia).

Remarkably, Pitney's "Only Love Can Break a Heart" was a No. 2 *Billboard* hit record at the same time that his penned recording "He's a Rebel" charted at No. 1 on *Billboard*. Thus, he had the top two hit records in the nation, one as a songwriter and one as a singer.

Very early in the 1960s, Pitney befriended the Rolling Stones. He became the first artist to cover a Jagger/Richards composition with the Top 10 UK hit "That Girl Belongs to Yesterday" (No. 7 in UK). It was also the first Jagger/Richards composition to make the U.S. charts (No. 49). On February 28, 1964, Gene performed "That Girl Belongs to Yesterday" on the popular British show *Ready, Steady, Go*. Also, Pitney played piano on the Stones' "Little by Little" and is acknowledged (along with Phil Spector) on the Stones' "Now I've Got a Witness" in the subtitle "Like Uncle Phil and Uncle Gene."

Gene Pitney was so popular that he was among the very few early U.S. 1960s artists who continued to enjoy hits after the British Invasion in 1964.

Pitney performed in a number of Connecticut music venues. His first performance ever was at the old Palace Theatre in his hometown of Rockville. Pitney performed in numerous other Connecticut music venues, including the Mohegan Sun, Foxwoods, the Actors Colony and more. The first concert for the 1967 Pitney tour was held in his home state of Connecticut at the Bushnell Memorial (August 1967). Pitney also performed a number of times on the *American Bandstand* TV show.

Gene Pitney was inducted into the Rock 'n' Roll Hall of Fame in 2002.

Throughout his entire life, Pitney stayed true to his home state of Connecticut. Aside from his sensational music career, Gene was highly regarded as a true family man and a down-to-earth person to his family, friends and legion of fans.

Gene Pitney passed away on April 5, 2006. The funeral service for Pitney was held at All Saints Church in Somersville on April 12, 2006. Included in the eulogy (given by a close friend) were references to several Pitney hit songs:

> For all of us baby boomers who as teenage boys cruised up and down Main Street, USA listening to "If I Only Had a Dime" or the countless teenage girls who cried at the foot of their bed listening to "Only Love Can Break a Heart," it is now time to say goodbye to Gene Pitney and say to ourselves "I'm Gonna Be Strong."

From the Coliseum to the Shaboo

Gene Pitney's high school yearbook photo. *Courtesy of the Vernon Historical Society.*

On October 19, 2016, Emily Santanella, on behalf of the Gene Pitney Commemorative Committee, paid tribute to a legend by dedicating a marble bench in memory of the great Gene Pitney. Here is a portion of Emily's presentation:

> *Today, I invite you to take a moment and really think about who he was. Listen to "I Wanna Love My Life Away" and marvel at the fact that he sang all of the harmonies and overdubbed instruments, something that has been called "a pioneering feat of record production." Listen to his songs in Spanish, Italian or German…because even in a foreign language, his voice will convey the emotion. Listen to his performance at Foxwoods in 2000 and appreciate the strength of his vocals, forty years after the start of his career. We all know that as a singer, songwriter and musician, he was incredibly talented. But let's also remember him as the man who held the door for you at the post office on Battle Street and who waved to let you turn ahead of him at an intersection, and who invited students interested in music careers to see his home studio through the high school's School to Career Program.*

The Gene Pitney Show (Tour)

> *Gene would always close the show with his hit song "I'm Gonna Be Strong." On one occasion, we were in a large gym and at the peak moment we sneaked on stage with whip cream pies and on the last note we all attacked Gene. It was hilarious, and the crowd loved it. The audience was in on the joke, as they watched it being set up, but Gene had no idea. The "Gene Pitney Show" was a great tour with a wonderful group of very talented artists.*
> —*Burton Stahl, of the Music Explosion*

HISTORIC CONNECTICUT MUSIC VENUES

Left: tour poster; *right*: group photo of artists on tour with the Gene Pitney Show, 1967. *Both courtesy of Ken Evans (of the Fifth Estate).*

In 1967, Gene Pitney headlined the Gene Pitney Show, which toured the U.S. that year. The first concert of the tour was at the Bushnell Memorial in Gene's home state of Connecticut. The performing acts in the Gene Pitney Show (in order of appearance) were Ronnie James Dio and the Prophets (opening act), the Music Explosion, the Fifth Estate, the Buckinghams, the Easybeats and the Happenings. Gene Pitney closed the show.

The D-Men

> *Prior to the name change of our band to the Fifth Estate, our group was known as the D-Men. The D-Men were the headline act at a 1964 performance at the Ezio Pinza music venue in Stamford, Connecticut. The Ezio Pinza was a three-thousand-seat outdoor amphitheater where many great artists performed over the years. This show was at the height of rock 'n' roll mania. When the show ended, the fans rushed the D-Men, who barely escaped intact.*
>
> —Ken Evans, of the Fifth Estate

Ken Evans (drummer for the D-Men and Fifth Estate) described the D-men in this way:

> *The D-Men band was known as a very good live band. We were a high-energy rock 'n' roll band. In every music venue we performed in, we felt a great deal of energy in the crowd and a real connection with our audience.*

We wrote our own material, and we were a very creative, independent band. Even before we changed our name to the Fifth Estate, the D-Men got a lot of radio airplay, especially in the Northeast. The D-Men had a very large local following. Our fan club consisted of thousands of fans from New York to New Haven. The local fans were fantastic and very supportive. At our first gig at Ezio Pinza Theatre in Stamford, the fans stormed the stage, which was very intense. This happened at other concerts also. We performed in a lot of music venues throughout the Northeast. We were also comfortable in the recording studio. We learned how to step up to the microphone and play our music straight through. Our band never needed a backup group or studio session musicians. So what you hear on the recordings was pretty much how we sounded in concert. We put out a lot of music, and we had no difficulty recording. In March 1965, The D-Men appeared on the popular national TV Show Hullabaloo, *cohosted by Brian Epstein and Michael Landon. Dionne Warwick was one of the performers on the show. If you look closely at the YouTube video, you will see that our band even got Michael Landon and Dionne Warwick dancing to our music!*

The Fifth Estate

The strength of our band was that we did things ourselves and in our own way. Whether it was the D-Men or the Fifth Estate bands, we did things on our own terms. Our sound evolved from surfing instrumentals in '63 to pop/rock tunes in '64 and edgier rock 'n' roll in '65, adding more R&B in '66 and adding more harpsichord and psych in '67. All without losing our rock 'n' roll dance band center ever—even today!
—*Ken Evans, of the D-Men and the Fifth Estate*

The Fifth Estate is a band that originated in Stamford. Wayne Wadhams (founding member), Ken Evans and Rick Engler all hailed from the Springdale section of Stamford. Bill Shute was from the Ridges section of Stamford. Doug Ferrara was from Stamford's Glenbrook section. Evans attended K.T. Murphy Grammar School and was a schoolmate of Jimmy Ienner (founding member of the Barons). Wadhams attended Stamford's Rippowam High, Ferrara went to Stamford High School and Evans and Engler attended Stamford Catholic High. Westport's Chuck Legros was also a band member briefly in 1966. Stamford's Bob Klein is a member of the reunited Fifth Estate band. He replaced Ken Evans in late 1969, when Ken took a hiatus from the group before eventually returning to the band. All group members grew up in proximity in Stamford neighborhoods, and they have always been close friends, kind of like brothers (somewhat unique since many bands split up and no longer retain the friendship they once had).

At a very early age, child prodigy Wadhams played the organ between movies at New Haven's Paramount Theater on Temple Street. In 1963, Wadhams enlisted Evans, Ferrara, Shute and Engler and formed a band called the Decadants. The group began as a garage/rock band that performed mainly in the Stamford area. The name of the band changed to the Demen and then to the D-Men. As the D-Men, the band signed with the United Artists/VEEP recording label and released three songs that were played on East Coast radio stations. The D-Men gained national attention when they performed their song "I Just Don't Care" on the popular national music variety TV show *Hullabaloo*. Ken Evans reminisced about an important radio contest held by famed WINS DJ Murray the K:

> *Murray the K had this weekly call-in contest on his famous WINS radio show. The fans were to call in and vote for their favorite bands. One week, the choice was between the Animals, the Dave Clark 5 and the D-Men. Because we had such a large following in New York City and Connecticut, all our fans called in and flooded the lines. So we won the contest. However, Murray the K felt that we had somehow "rigged" the contest (which we didn't), and he stopped playing our songs. The funny thing about all of this is that later on when our songs like "The Witch Is Dead" hit it really big in New York, Murray the K loved them and played them constantly, not knowing that the Fifth Estate was really the D-Men band that he had previously banned on his station!*

The band changed their name to the Fifth Estate in 1965. In 1967, the Fifth Estate had a major international hit with their signature song "Ding Dong! The Witch Is Dead," a tune that peaked at No. 11 on the *Billboard* charts. In Connecticut, "Ding Dong! The Witch Is Dead" was a No. 1 hit record and also a No. 1 hit in other parts of the country. The Fifth Estate even sang the song in five different languages, which appealed to countries outside the United States. "Ding Dong! The Witch Is Dead" has been described as "a creative merge of rock and classical baroque."

The band actually had hits all over the world. For example, "Morning" was a hit record in Australia; "Heigh Ho" was a Top 40 song in Canada.

From the Coliseum to the Shaboo

"That's Love" was big in Brazil. And believe it or not, their songs were a hit in Turkey and other places not associated with rock music, at least at that time.

The Fifth Estate's Ken "Furvus" Evans describes the Connecticut music scene in this way:

> *There always was a good, solid rock base in Connecticut. Many people don't understand that. Connecticut was a great "proving ground" for rock 'n' roll groups. Bands like ours liked the fact that Connecticut was located close to the large radio markets in New York, New Jersey and Massachusetts. Connecticut has always been a good place to "earn your chops."*

In 1967, the Fifth Estate band toured throughout the United States as part of the Gene Pitney Show. The band also toured the states with other recording artists such as the Turtles and the Lovin' Spoonful.

There is a connection between the Fifth Estate and the rock band AC/DC, as described by Ken Evans:

> *Harry Vanda and George Young of the Easybeats were also coproducers of the early AC/DC albums. (We toured with the EasyBeats for months.) George is the brother of AC/DC's Angus Young. I knew Harry and George very well and had dinner with them many times. At one such dinner, they mentioned that they were inspired by the Fifth Estate's use of bagpipes in our song "Do Drop Inn." Because of this, they decided to incorporate*

Left: The Fifth Estate standing at the entrance to Alan Freed's Greycliff Manor residence in Stamford, Connecticut, 1966. *Left to right*: Wayne Wadhams, Chuck Legros, Bill Shute, Rick Engler, Ken Evans and Doug Ferrara. *Right*: The D-Men on the *Hullabaloo* TV Show. *Both courtesy of Ken Evans.*

bagpipes in AC/DC's hit rock anthem "It's a Long Way to the Top (If You Wanna Rock 'n' Roll)." They got that right! It surely is!

Throughout the years, the Fifth Estate has proven to be a multitalented band and covered a number of music genres, including rock, pop, folk/rock and classical baroque. The band has performed in numerous music venues with noted artists such as Gene Pitney, the Bluebeats, the Wildweeds, the Barons and the Shags.

In 2004, the group reunited. Since then, the band has released a number of albums. Two of the albums were coproduced by Ken Evans and famed producer Shel Talmy (who produced the Kinks, the Who and the Easybeats).

The Fifth Estate's newest album (released May 1, 2020) is called *Garunge Deluxe*, a nice compilation of the band's rock 'n' roll recordings over the years.

Interesting facts:

- Ken Evans managed the popular Connecticut band the Reducers in the 1980s.
- The Highwaymen folk group recorded a song cowritten by Wayne Wadhams. The song was also recorded by the Fifth Estate.

The Fifth Estate band is planning to release a new album by the end of March 2022. More information can be found on: www.thefifthestateband.com.

The Who

The Who performed at the Bushnell on November 4, 1969.

The Shags

The Shags formed in West Haven, Connecticut, in 1965. The cofounders of the Shags were Carl Augusto and Tom Violante. The two were schoolmates at West Haven's Notre Dame High School.

In November 1964, Augusto and Violante formed a group called the Hollywood High Drop Outs (HHDO). Two members of the HHDO (Carl Augusto and Johnny Tangredi) had left another group called the Deltons to join the HHDO.

The HHDO lineup that ultimately became the Shags featured Carl Augusto, Tom Violante, Johnny Tangredi and Billy Hall. Note: Carl, Tom and Johnny took stage names: Carl "Donnell," Tommy "Roberts" and Johnny "Stanton," respectively. Like many groups, HHDO had different incarnations.

In 1965, the HHDO band changed its name to the Shags. Also, in 1965, the Shags recorded their first single, "Wait and See," with the B side "It Hurts Me Bad." Both sides were hits on the local charts. "Wait and See" became a No. 5 hit in Connecticut. "Don't Press Your Luck" was one of the best-known songs by the Shags. The song is featured on the popular Sundazed double LP/CD release *Don't Press Your Luck! The IN Sound of 60s Connecticut*. The group's cover of the Beatles' "I Call Your Name" was also a popular song and received national attention.

A bit of trivia: Orrin Bolotin (Michael Bolton's brother) was a Shags roadie. Michael got to know the members of the Shags and asked Carl Augusto to teach him how to play guitar.

In 1966, the Shags were selected to appear on the pilot of a New Haven TV show (WNHC/WTNH) called *The Show with the Very Long Title*. Also appearing with the Shags on this scheduled TV pilot were the Bram Rigg Set. However, the show was never aired.

One of the highlights for the group was in 1968 when the Shags performed on their own at the Oakdale Theatre and nearly sold out the theater, with 3,400 of the 3,600 seats filled. The Shags opened for major artists in Connecticut music venues, including Simon & Garfunkel, the Rascals, Gene Pitney, Dion, Righteous Brothers and B.B. King. In addition, the Shags performed at the Bushnell Memorial and were one of the featured bands at the Teen Tempo '66 show in Milford.

As a tribute to the band's popularity, a plaque honoring the Shags is displayed in the basement of New Haven's St. Bernadette Church, alongside the Five Satins' plaque.

THE SHABOO INN (SHABOO STAGE)

I was the luckiest guy in America to own and run the Shaboo Inn. It was such a thrill and honor to bring all these amazing artists to my town and enable the fans to have so much joy. Truly, I was the luckiest kid in the country. I wouldn't trade that experience for anything. It's just like Mike

Finnigan wrote in his song "What A Life"—"I wouldn't swap [my life] with anybody—not even BB's or Lightning's or Muddy's."

And to think that so many years later, the Shaboo Spirit lives on with the construction of the new Shaboo Stage. Truly remarkable.

—David "Lefty" Foster, former owner of the Shaboo Inn and member of the Shaboo All-Stars

"Lefty" Foster, his brother Mark, my sister Kerry, my late brother Gary and I are truly honored and humbled that you have all kept alive the Shaboo name and spirit for all of these years. Shaboo was always more about all of you (the many fans and artists) than it was us. It was a true communal journey and we were honored just to steer the ship.

—Bruce John, former owner of the Shaboo Inn

The Shaboo was a Class A music venue, run by Class A people. When I was with NRBQ, we played there many many times. The Shaboo was a wooden structure that had great sound acoustics. The reaction of the fans to our music was awesome. It was the perfect place to play at the time. A lot of college kids would come out to hear some really great music. It would get so crowded that it was hard to breathe sometimes, and we felt squished trying to get off the stage. And, man, it got so hot in there from all the people wanting to get close to the stage. Of course, they sold a lot of beer because of that!

Everybody wanted to play at the Shaboo, and it seemed like everyone did. Artists like Bonnie Raitt would stay overnight just to see us play, which was very cool. Taj Mahal played there a number of times. He was my idol back then—still is.

Because NRBQ was such a good draw, they would put us on later and later at night. Same thing happened to us at Toad's Place.

The Shaboo Inn had a really nice vibe, and everyone had a good time there.

—Al Anderson, of the Wildweeds, NRBQ

I played the Shaboo in September 1977. Such a great venue! As a solo artist, the Shaboo Inn was one of those places instrumental in getting my solo recordings promoted and advertised. Places like that were really important to me. I would introduce certain songs that I wrote in venues like the Shaboo, build a fan following, and get fan reaction—hopefully favorable reaction.

—Felix Cavaliere

Left: The Shaboo Inn; *right*: The Shaboo stage. *Both courtesy of David "Lefty" Foster.*

The Shaboo Inn in Mansfield, Connecticut, was founded by David "Lefty" Foster and Bruce John in 1971. Foster was only nineteen, and John was barely twenty years old. Tragically, the Shaboo Inn closed in 1982 and burned down to the ground soon after.

During its eleven-year run, the Shaboo became one of the premier music venues in the Northeast, hosting nearly three thousand concerts. Sold-out concerts at the Shaboo were frequent occurrences as the capacity crowd of one thousand fans were treated to many amazing performances by their favorite bands. The legendary artists and bands that performed at the Shaboo include Muddy Waters, Bonnie Raitt, Felix Cavaliere, Joe Cocker, B.B. King, James Cotton, Taj Mahal, Richie Havens, the Talking Heads, Jimmy Buffett, Miles Davis, Buddy Rich, the Reducers, Rick Derringer, Johnny Winter, José Feliciano, Journey, Elvis Costello, Lou Reed, the Police, Edgar Winter and many, many more.

Even though the Shaboo Inn no longer exists, the "Shaboo Spirit" lives on. Thanks to the David "Lefty" Foster Family Foundation, a beautiful new stage was erected in Willimantic's Jillson Square in 2018. The new stage was fittingly named in honor of the Shaboo Inn. The Shaboo Stage has been the site of a number of special concerts such as the August 3, 2018 inaugural Shaboo Stage concert with José Feliciano and a tribute to Woodstock's fiftieth anniversary (featuring performances by Canned Heat, NRBQ and David "Lefty" Foster's Shaboo All-Stars).

The celebration of the fiftieth anniversary of Shaboo Inn was held at the Shaboo Stage on August 28, 2021. The list of scheduled performers included Pure Prairie League, Tom Rush, NRBQ and David "Lefty" Foster's Shaboo All Stars. Over three thousand fans were in attendance.

Other notable performances at the Shaboo Inn:

Aerosmith

In 1971, Aerosmith debuted "Dream On," which soon became a mega-hit for the band, at the Shaboo Inn.

Steven Tyler of Aerosmith. *Copyright Ivor Levene.*

NRBQ with "Big Al" Anderson

NRBQ with "Big Al" Anderson performed at the Shaboo Inn well over twenty-five times.

NRBQ's Al Anderson with Henry McNulty. *Courtesy of Henry McNulty.*

José Feliciano

There's so many great musicians in Connecticut. This state has a tremendous history.

—*José Feliciano*

International recording star José Feliciano and his wife, Susan, have been residents of Weston, Connecticut, since 1990. Feliciano's achievements include forty-five Gold/Platinum records, nineteen Grammy nominations and nine Grammys.

His rendition of "Light My Fire" reached No. 3 in the United States (and No. 1 in Canada and the United Kingdom). The song was a major hit on Connecticut radio stations. Feliciano's "Feliz Navidad" has become a holiday classic. During the time he has been a Connecticut resident, Feliciano has recorded over twenty singles and albums in English and Spanish.

Feliciano was the featured artist at the grand opening of the newly reconstructed Levitt Pavilion in Westport on Sunday, July 20, 2014, and he has also performed in various other Connecticut music venues, including the Oakdale Theatre (five times) and the Shaboo Stage.

On January 16, 2014, José Feliciano was one of ten famous Connecticut musicians honored by the Fairfield Museum and History Center at an event referred to as Fairfield's Rockin' Top 10. In a *Connecticut Post* article by Scott Gargan on March 27, 2014, Feliciano was asked how it felt to be celebrated as one of the region's most influential musicians (as one of Fairfield's Rockin' Top 10). José Feliciano responded, "It's a wonderful thing. I never thought I'd be included. There's so many great musicians in Connecticut. This state has a tremendous history."

Peter Tork

Singer, songwriter, actor and musician Peter Tork was a resident of Mansfield, Connecticut. Tork (born Peter Halsten Thorkelson) is best remembered as a member of the extremely popular group the Monkees. He was known as the "Court Jester" of the Monkees.

The Thorkelson family moved to Storrs-Mansfield when Peter was seven years old to enable his father, Halsten Thorkelson, to become an economics professor at the University of Connecticut–Storrs. Peter attended Windham High School (Willimantic) and graduated from E.O. Smith High School in Storrs-Mansfield, class of 1959. E.O. Smith is the same high school that Rivers Cuomo (of Weezer) attended years later.

Tork was an accomplished musician and learned the piano when he was a young child growing up in Mansfield. He became proficient at other instruments, such as bass guitar, acoustic guitar, banjo and harpsichord.

Throughout the years, Tork recorded many songs both with the Monkees and as a solo artist. He was a member of several bands (for example, the Shoe Suede Blues band) and performed with major recording artists George Harrison and Jimi Hendrix. On his website, www.petertork.com, Tork noted that Hendrix referred to him as "the most talented Monkee." Peter also reunited, recorded

Peter Tork. *Copyright Ivor Levene.*

and toured several times with his former Monkees bandmates. Besides his television work with the Monkees, he landed roles in several TV sitcoms.

Tork played in many music venues in Connecticut, including the Shaboo Inn, E.O. Smith High School (his alma mater), Stamford High School, UCONN Storrs and spots in Middletown and Lebanon, Connecticut.

After graduating from high school in Connecticut, Peter Tork moved a number of times around the country before returning home to Mansfield.

Peter Tork passed away on February 21, 2019. He was cremated, and his ashes were scattered out to sea.

Village Maid Band

The Village Maid Band was composed of former members of two popular Connecticut bands: Little Village and Arizona Maid Band (AMB). Bernie Palka (drums) played with both Little Village and AMB. Michael "Mick" Niewwinski (bass) was from AMB. Victor Cowles (guitar, vocals) also played with AMB.

Little Village was a hard rock band from the Hartford area. The band was popular in the Connecticut region and performed at Connecticut music venues such as the Shaboo Inn (six times) and New Haven's Palace Theatre.

The Arizona Maid Band formed in 1973, and group members hailed from the Connecticut towns of Somers, Ellington, Stafford Springs, South Windsor and Enfield. AMB played mainly southern rock music. Among the music venues that the band performed in was the Shaboo Inn. The Arizona Maid Band was popular on a local/regional basis.

WOOLSEY HALL

A gorgeous, ornate classical hall. An incredible cultural outlet.
—*Yale newsletter*

Woolsey Hall is a 2,650-seat music venue located at the corner of New Haven's College and Grove Streets. Built for Yale University's bicentennial celebration in 1901, Woolsey Hall has hosted numerous recording artists. Woolsey Hall was named in honor of Theodore Dwight Woolsey, president of Yale from 1846 through 1871.

From the Coliseum to the Shaboo

Woolsey Hall, Yale (front view). *Library of Congress.*

The following are some of the artists that performed at Woolsey Hall:

Jimi Hendrix Concert: November 17, 1968

I have vivid memories of the Jimi Hendrix Experience concert at Woolsey Hall. Hendrix was just riveting. There he was with Mitch Mitchell on drums and Noel Redding on bass. I knew they were going to be loud, but I had no idea how loud. Whenever Hendrix hit his wah-wah foot pedal, it was absolutely ear-shattering. Jimi opened with "Sgt. Pepper's Lonely Hearts Club Band" and quickly segued into "Fire." He closed with "Purple Haze." I clearly remember those white boots with his pants tucked in and the scarf tied around his leg. I believe he had worn the fringe jacket in the first show, but he had removed it for the second concert. Hendrix did a lot of his trademark moves, playing behind his neck, and at times seemingly with his teeth. An unforgettable experience. It was the only time I would get to see Hendrix play live. Two years later, I was devastated by the news of his death. One of the true greats was taken from us. Soon there would be more.
—Paul Rosano, *of Pulse and Napi Browne*

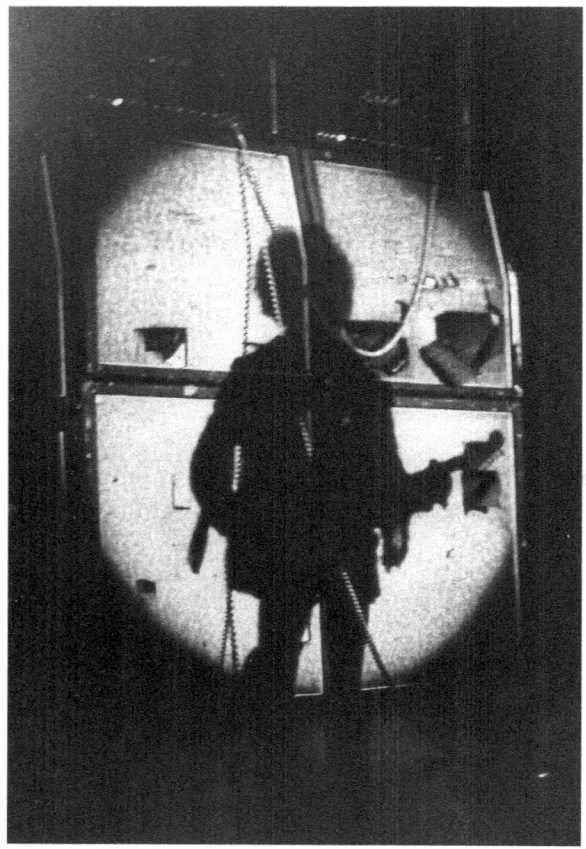

Joe Sia's iconic photo of Jimi Hendrix at New Haven's Woolsey Hall on November 17, 1968. *Author's collection, received directly from Joe Sia and signed, dated and numbered by Sia. Image used with permission from wolfgangsvault (Bill Sagan).*

Perhaps the most memorable performances at Woolsey Hall were the two concerts by Jimi Hendrix on November 17, 1968. The fans at Woolsey Hall were in total awe of Hendrix's musicianship, especially his scorching and electrifying guitar. Wearing his feathered boots and buckskin jacket, Hendrix closed out his show by smashing his guitar on the historic stage floor and against his amplifiers. He topped it all off by lighting his guitar on fire and leaving the stage, much to the delight of the Woolsey Hall fans.

In the words of famed rock photographer Joe Sia, live performances by Hendrix were "spellbinding." Joe would know, since Hendrix was one of his favorite photographic subjects, and as a result, he became close to this important artist. Sia's iconic photo of Jimi Hendrix at Woolsey Hall has been showcased in print media as well as album cover art.

Sia's chronicle of the original Woodstock Festival has earned the praise of many people, including his peers, who consider it the premier photographic account of this historically important music event. In a tribute to Joe, his alma mater (Sacred Heart University) discussed his impressive career in a university newsletter:

> *Few photographers have made a more indelible imprint in the world of rock music than Joe Sia. Joe's photographs capture the essence of a performer's style and reflect the rhythms of the artist's music. Sia is one of the most widely published people in his profession.*

Famed rock photographer Joe Sia (1945–2003) at Fairfield's Sacred Heart University (his alma mater). *SHU Yearbook photo.*

The Supremes

The legendary female group the Supremes consisted of Connecticut resident Diana Ross, Mary Wilson and Florence Ballard. Previously formed as the Primates in Detroit in 1959, their name was changed to the Supremes when they signed with Motown in 1960. The Supremes had twelve No. 1 recordings. Most of the Supremes' hits were written and produced by the legendary songwriting team of Holland-Dozier-Holland.

The Supremes performed at Woolsey Hall on March 5, 1965. They also played at other Connecticut music venues such as the Bushnell Memorial, the New Haven Arena and the University of Bridgeport. The first appearance of the Supremes in Connecticut was at the New Haven Arena on November 3, 1962, prior to achieving their amazing success as a trio. The Supremes were inducted into the Rock 'n' Roll Hall of Fame in 1988.

Bonnie Raitt

> *I think my fans will follow me into our combined old age. Real musicians and real fans stay together for a long, long time.*
> —*Bonnie Raitt*

> *Bonnie Raitt is the best! She's in it for the music. That's it. I had three songs on her comeback album and went on tour with Bonnie.*
> —*Al Anderson, musician/songwriter*

Bonnie Raitt is a multi–Grammy Award singer, songwriter, and noted guitarist. In 1989, her outstanding album *Nick of Time* won three Grammy Awards, including Album of the Year.

Bonnie performed at Woolsey Hall on February 23, 1973. Raitt also played at other Connecticut music venues, including the Shaboo Inn (four times), Oakdale Theatre (four times), Mohegan Sun, Foxwoods, Toad's Place and The Meadows Music Theatre.

Jasper Wrath

Jasper Wrath was an extremely popular progressive rock band in the New Haven area. The 1975 song "You" was written by band members Jeff Cannata and Michael Soldan and was a No. 1 song in the New Haven region. "Did You Know That" also charted well in the greater New Haven area.

Jasper Wrath formed in 1969 in Hamden. The band was founded by Cannata and Robert Giannotti. The other original members of the band were Soldan and Phil Stone. Also joining the band were James Christian, Scott Zito and Jeff Batter. Jasper Wrath disbanded in 1976. Jasper Wrath performed at a number of the concerts at New Haven's Yale University.

Jasper Wrath at New Haven's Yale University campus. *Courtesy of Jeff Cannata.*

From the Coliseum to the Shaboo

THE SHACK

In high school, I played in a band called the Flares. I remember playing at the Shack several times around 1966–67. It was a great venue, with low ceilings, wood floors, and a low stage set in one corner. Packed with dancing teenagers, it was the place to be on Friday night!
—Ray Lamitola, of South Michigan Avenue and the Flares

The Shack was on Buckingham Street in Oakville. It is now a church. Kind of ironic since we used to worship rock 'n' roll in that same building. You entered on the side, up a staircase. The room was, I'm guessing, thirty by one hundred with benches attached to the walls; the bandstand was in the corner opposite the entrance. The Adler Bros ran the place and always said just bring in the Wildweeds once a month and you'll do fine.
—Lou Rizzuti

When I think of the Shack, I recall how the floor would shake while we were dancing. I was afraid we were gonna fall through it!
—Kathy Barbino Mosgrove

Former location site of the Shack. *Courtesy of Kathy Barbino Mosgrove.*

HISTORIC CONNECTICUT MUSIC VENUES

The Shack was a popular fun music venue that was located on 500 Buckingham Street in Oakville (across from Polk School).

The following are a few of the artists that performed at the Shack (Oakville):

The Wildweeds

For Connecticut residents growing up in the 1960s, the Wildweeds (of Windsor, Connecticut) were one of the most popular and admired bands from their state.

The band's 1967 song "No Good to Cry" was certainly a fan favorite among Connecticut residents and has become a cult classic. Even to this day, the mere mention of "No Good to Cry" will put a smile on the face of many baby boomers who grew up listening and dancing to the song in the 1960s. The record received extensive airplay throughout the Northeast region and was the No. 1 song on Connecticut radio stations. The tune charted No. 15 on WWCO's Top 100 songs for the year 1967. The song also fared very well in other markets in the United States, such as New Orleans (No. 5), Cleveland (No. 5) and many areas in the South. While "No Good to Cry" did make the national charts (No. 87), the feeling (at least in the Connecticut area) was that the song deserved a much better fate. Given the enormous popularity of the song in the regions mentioned, many people are still bewildered as to why the tune never achieved greater national success or became a major hit for the band.

The Wildweeds (aka the Weeds) recorded at Doc Cavalier's Syncron Studios (later named Trod Nossel Studios) in Wallingford.

The band members included Al Anderson (lead vocals, guitar), Ray Zeiner (keyboards, vocals), Bob Dudek (bass, vocals), Skip Yakaitis (percussion, vocals) and Andy Lepak (drums). Later, Jeff Potter joined the group. The Wildweeds used musicians from Hartford's Hartt School of Music on some of their recordings.

The band's follow-up songs included "Someday Morning," "It Was Fun (While It Lasted)," "And When She Smiles" and "I'm Dreaming." These songs were Top 10 hits in Connecticut. Also, the Wildweeds album *The Wildweeds Greatest Hits & More* was very popular in the Connecticut area. As was the case with "No Good to Cry," the follow-up singles did well in

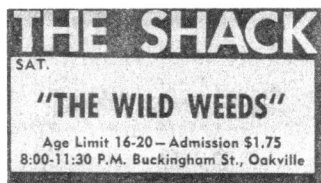

Top: Ad for Wildweeds at the Shack. *Bottom*: The Wildweeds setting up for their performance at the Shack (Oakville), June 15, 1968. *Both courtesy of Mary Beth Welsh.*

the Northeast and in other markets around the country. (For example, "And When She Smiles" was a Top 10 hit in Tulsa, Oklahoma.) Several of these songs appeared on *Billboard*'s "bubbling under" charts.

The Wildweeds shared the stage with Jim Morrison and the Doors for two sold-out concerts at the Oakdale Theatre on September 23–24, 1967. When asked how his first meeting went with the members of the Doors, "Big" Al responded, "When I walked into the Doors dressing room, I noticed that none of the Doors were talking to each other, so I walked out." They also shared the stage with other Connecticut bands such as Stamford's Fifth Estate. In addition to the Oakdale, the Weeds also performed in a number of other Connecticut music venues, including The Shack and the Cheri Shack.

At the end of 1971, Al Anderson joined NRBQ and became an integral part of that great band. He has also had a successful solo career. "Big Al" now is one of the most sought-after songwriters because of the many hit songs he has written for other recording artists. Also, after the Wildweeds, Ray Zeiner's "I Had a Girl" charted at No. 14 on Waterbury's WWCO on February 4, 1972.

The Wildweeds reunited on several occasions in recent years. Christine Ohlman performed with a reunited Wildweeds band in their 2011, 2014 and 2015 concerts. Ohlman sang the harmony parts of the Wildweeds' Bob Dudek. She has had a long association with Al Anderson and the Wildweeds. Christine, along with her band the Wrongh Black Bag, had opened for the Wildweeds very early in her career.

Pulse (aka the Pulse)

In August 1967, the Pulse came together as a merger of two popular Connecticut rock bands: the Shags and the Bram Rigg Set (BRS). This new group consisted of the Shags' Carl Augusto "Donnell," Tom Violante "Roberts," Lance Gardiner and the Bram Rigg Set's Beau Segal, Peter Neri and Rich Bednarczyk.

In January 1968, the band's name was changed to Pulse. There were also personnel changes. Pulse now consisted of Segal, Neri, Bednarczyk, Donnell, Jeff Potter and Paul Rosano. Pulse played its first gig at Oakville's the Shack. During their career, the band opened for major recording artists such as the Lovin' Spoonful. "Another Woman" by Pulse was written by Rosano and charted No. 52 on New Haven radio in 1969.

"My Old Boy" was a No. 52 hit in Springfield, Massachusetts. Pulse was managed by Doc Cavalier, owner of Syncron Recording Studios (later called Trod Nossel). The group disbanded at the end of 1970. After Pulse, Paul Rosano joined the Connecticut band Napi Browne. The original Pulse album has recently been remastered and includes bonus tracks. Pulse was a very popular blues-rock group, known for live performances and rock album compositions.

The Flares

> *I'm just a typical small-time musician. I guess my story is similar to many others throughout the United States who wanted to play in a band just for the love of it. I started a long time ago, went through a lot of phases, worked hard at it, played with a lot of good musicians, and loved doing it. I always considered myself to be a decent musician. I never thought I was in the same category as some of the greats from our state and never pretended to be anything other than what I am. I'm just proud to be among the many thousands of good musicians that came out of Connecticut.*
> —Ray Lamitola

The Flares were a rock cover band formed in 1964 by Mario Infanti in the Town Plot section of Waterbury, Connecticut. The band played mainly in dance clubs in Waterbury and surrounding areas, such as

The Flares. *Courtesy of Ray Lamitola of the Flares, South Michigan Avenue.*

Oakville's the Shack. The band consisted of Mario Infanti (lead guitar, vocals), Ray Lamitola (rhythm guitar, vocals), Carmen Farino (drums) and Ron Migliarise (bass). After the Flares dissolved in 1967, Ray Lamitola joined South Michigan Avenue, a rock band formed by Jerry Roraback (drummer). South Michigan Avenue was a popular cover band known for fine renditions of songs by groups like Grand Funk Railroad, Santana and CCR. Band members Thom Serrani, Jerry Rorabach and Ray Lamitola attended Sacred Heart University in Fairfield. Years later, Serrani became the mayor of Stamford. Also, Roraback has sat in with several well-known acts such as the Happenings.

Hullabaloo

Ah, the Hullabaloo and the Shack—two dance places that were a big part of the local high-school kids in the late '60s. We would go to Hullabaloo on Friday night and the Shack on Saturday night

For those of us who attended, if you close your eyes and think hard enough you can hear the Righteous Brother's song "Unchained Melody" or songs from The Temptations. I would pick up a carload of friends in my 1963 Chevy Convertible, go to the dance, then head out to Big Top on Watertown Avenue and grab a burger and soda. We would just hang out until it was time to get the kids home before curfew. Just being together with friends—no cellphones, tablets, smartphones, just each other's company; lots of laughs and fun. Imagine a time of music, dancing, friends and just being yourself. Too bad the kids of today don't know what they are missing.
—*Jackie Cipriano*

Hullabaloo was in the old Ice Palace on Thomaston Ave in Waterbury. It had bleachers on either side with three or four rows on both bleachers. The stage for performers was at the very end.
—*Lou Rizzuti*

We all loved Hullabaloo! It was a place for all the local teenagers to dance, listen to some great music and have fun. It was very dark inside. If you wore a white shirt, the blue light made it look bright white. I loved that. The music venue catered to teenagers. Alcoholic beverages were not allowed. I actually saved one of the paper cups after I finished a Coca-Cola. It had

Historic Connecticut Music Venues

Left: Former location site of Hullabaloo. *Courtesy of Kathy Barbino Mosgrove.*

Right: Vanilla Fudge at Hullabaloo's Grand Opening in Waterbury. *Author's collection.*

> the fancy Hullabaloo logo on it, and I put the date on the bottom (February 17, 1967). I still have the Hullabaloo cup to this day. It was such an innocent time, and we had a blast there.
>
> —*Kathy (Barbino) Mosgrove*

The Hullabaloo was located on Thomaston Avenue in Waterbury, Connecticut. This music venue was a popular dance spot for local teenagers.

Yesterday's Children

Yesterday's Children (aka the Children) hailed from the Cheshire, Prospect and Waterbury areas and formed in 1966. The band's music style was garage rock, psych and hard rock. The 1966 single "To Be or Not to Be" was popular in Connecticut and a Top 40 hit on major Connecticut radio stations (WPOP, WWCO and others). The tune charted at No. 41 on WWCO's Top 100 songs for 1967. The recording also did well in several other markets. (It was a Top 30 hit in Flint, Michigan.)

The band's self-titled *Yesterday's Children* album received good reviews. The Children's single and album are viewed by some as cult classics, especially in the garage/punk circles. "To Be or Not to Be" also appeared on the compilation album *Psychedelic Unknowns Volume 2*. Yesterday's Children regularly played at music venues in Connecticut, such as Waterbury's Hullabaloo and the Actors Colony. The group disbanded in 1969.

From the Coliseum to the Shaboo

THE CHERI SHACK

In the late 1960s, I had the notion to start the first disco ever in Connecticut at my father's Bill Miller's Dance Village in Branford, Connecticut. I was teaching ballet and modern dance there and he ran trampoline and gymnastic classes. My father told me three times that the disco would never work, but I finally wore him down. The disco was so much fun, and I participated as a go-go dancer at times. It certainly was an inventive time!

We were very creative at Cheri Shack. For example, we would fill a weather balloon with smoke and when it popped, the smoke would fill the room. We featured professional lighting (black lights). I painted the dancers' legs with stripes, so the black light just illuminated two pairs of striped legs and no bodies. We also featured strobe lighting. When we turned on the strobe flash lighting, it made you feel like you were in a thundercloud. My brother had dry ice haze pouring like a waterfall from a beam over the stage.

The ballroom would get so tightly packed that police would admit a person only if another was exiting. The Cheri Shack was an extremely popular and fun music venue.

—Cheri Miller Weymann

When Bill Miller opened the Cheri Shack in Branford, it was by far the most beautiful "teen" room, with its dark, barnwood interior, exposed beams, and stained glass. Miller was a visionary who would, in later years, expand the Cheri Shack into a huge castle-like structure complete with towers, turrets, and several outdoor gazebos. There was a thriving music scene there for the bands of the day, including my own Wrongh Black Bag, helmed by my brother, Vic Steffens. Bill's daughter, Cheri, the club's namesake, was known to go-go dance, on occasion, with a giant snake that was kept in a glass case in the dressing room. All in all, a MUCH more exotic (and memorable!) scene than what was going on in the other clubs of the day!

—Christine Ohlman

I played there often with Pulse '68 to '69 and then with The Wildweeds in '70 to '71. Cheri was the daughter of the owner, Bill Miller. Cheri would go-go dance, and on occasion, she danced with a boa constrictor while the bands played. The walls were lined with mirrors, and Pulse's lead singer was legally blind, although he could function and still get around on stage at that time. (He later became president of the American Foundation for the

Cheri Miller Weymann of the Cheri Shack. *Courtesy of the* Shoreline Times.

The Cheri Shack was located in the building to the left of the big tower of windows. *Courtesy of Cheri Miller Weyman.*

Blind.) As he left the stage, I saw him heading towards a mirrored wall. Well, he walked right into it, which surprised a few that didn't know he had vision problems. I didn't have time to stop him.
—Jeff Potter, of Pulse and the Wildweeds

The Cheri Shack in Branford was simply the best club in the New Haven area, if not one of the best venues in state. Inside Bill Miller's Dance Studio on Route 1 was a beautiful, rustic, shingled building (which still stands by the way) that looked like a huge upscaled barn. The club was directly to the right when you entered. It was, in fact, a dance studio with a gorgeous hardwood floor and ballet mirror and bar on the left the length of the long room. The stage was at the far end of the room, a good size, not oversized, with spots for dancers. There was also a balcony with tables accessible from a staircase at the back left. Friday and Saturday nights always saw packed audiences, there to listen and dance. Pulse played there many times, I believe about once a month at one point, and it was always a great experience.
—Paul Rosano, of Pulse and the Bram Rigg Set

I always really liked playing at Cheri Shack. At one point, we opened for Sopwith Camel when they were on tour with their hit, "Hello, Hello." These guys were grown men with their wives or partners (or groupies). I felt like we were so young in comparison—because we were young! It must have been around 1966 or 1967 (which would have made us about seventeen years old).
—Peter Neri, of Pulse and the Bram Rigg Set

Before renaming our band Bridge, our group was known as the Symbolix. We played in music venues all over the New Haven area, including the Trapezoid, the House of Zodiac and, of course, the place everyone loved to play, the Cheri Shack.
—Dennis D'Amato, of the Symbolix and Bridge

As noted in her quote, Cheri Miller convinced her father (Bill Miller) that the Shoreline needed its own discotheque—as Cheri alleges, "the first disco ever in Connecticut."

In the days before computers, Cheri would make up her own flyers by hand and distribute them all over to promote the Cheri Shack, located in Branford. Cheri noted, "I would distribute flyers to all the students

Left: Cheri Shack's Cheri Miller go-go dancing while Michael Bolton (then known as Michael Bolotin) sings. *Right*: Handmade flyer for Cheri Shack (pre-computer days). *Both courtesy of Cheri Miller Weyman.*

who attended Branford High School." Her efforts paid off, resulting in a packed house at her venue on a regular basis. The Cheri Shack featured "a Groovy Atmosphere; Three go-go girls; A music venue run by teenagers for teenagers; and 'ear-resistible' bands." Cheri herself was one of the go-go girls on occasion.

In the 1960s, the Cheri Shack was an extremely popular dance club for teenagers. Cheri Miller had a lot to do with making the club a huge success.

Cheri's father made significant additions to the structure, and the venue is now a family-owned banquet facility known as Bill Miller's Castle.

The following are some of the artists who performed at the Cheri Shack:

The Wildweeds

The Wildweeds of Windsor, Connecticut, performed several times at the Cheri Shack.

From the Coliseum to the Shaboo

The Pulse (aka Pulse)

North Atlantic Invasion Force (NAIF)

The North Atlantic Invasion Force (aka NAIF) was formed in West Haven in 1964 by lead singer-songwriter George Morgio. A number of their songs were hits on the local charts in Connecticut, and a few were regional hits. The NAIF's biggest song was "Black on White," recorded in 1966 and released in 1968. "Black on White" became the No. 1 song in parts of Connecticut (thanks in part to WAVZ). It appeared on the national music charts and was successful in several different markets in the United States (No. 2 song in Flint, Michigan, and a popular tune in Detroit, parts of Kentucky and so on). The song was even played on the nationally televised show *American Bandstand*. NAIF was the opening act for many major recording bands. NAIF performed in a number of Connecticut music venues, including the very popular Cheri Shack.

Advertisement for Pulse band at Cheri Shack. *Courtesy of Paul Rosano.*

THE INDIAN NECK FOLK FESTIVAL (THE MONTOWESE HOUSE)

The Montowese House in Branford, Connecticut, built in 1866, was the largest summer hotel between New York City and Newport. By the 1950s, it hosted elegant dinners, dances, Yale events and bridge tournaments. Later, the Montowese House became an indelible part of music history when it hosted the Indian Neck Folk Festival. The folk festival at the Montowese House attracted many of the country's most notable folk singers of the era, including Bob Dylan in 1961 and the Highwaymen folk group in 1960. The Montowese House closed in 1963.
    —Jane Bouley, Branford town historian, Branford Historical Society

The Indian Neck Folk Festival in Branford was an important music venue that holds a special place in music history. The festival there attracted many

The Montowese House (aka "The Queen of the Sound"). *Courtesy of the Branford Historical Society.*

of the leading folk singers of the time. It was there that a relatively unknown teenager by the name of Bob Dylan performed three Woody Guthrie songs outside the Montowese House as part of the Indian Neck Folk Festival. The date of this event was May 6, 1961. The audio of his performance in Branford is believed to be the earliest Bob Dylan audio recordings. You might say this was Bob Dylan before *the* Bob Dylan.

A year earlier, this same venue served as a launching pad for five Wesleyan University students who were just gaining popularity on the folk scene. The group was called the Highwaymen, and the members' performance in the Montowese House drew a large crowd as part of the Indian Neck Folk Festival. The quintet had just recorded a song to be released several months later that would become a huge No. 1 *Billboard* hit. The song was called "Michael, Row the Boat Ashore."

The following are some of the artists who performed at the Indian Neck Folk Festival (Montowese House):

From the Coliseum to the Shaboo

Bob Dylan

Bob Dylan performed at the Indian Neck Folk Festival (outside the Montowese House) on May 6, 1961.

Left: A rare photo of Bob Dylan performing at the Indian Neck Folk Festival in Branford, Connecticut, on May 6, 1961. *Photo by Joe Alper, courtesy of Joe Alper Photo Collection, LLC.*

Below: The Highwaymen performing in the Montowese House as part of the Indian Neck Folk Festival on May 7, 1960. *Photo by Earl Colter, courtesy of the Branford Historical Society.*

Historic Connecticut Music Venues

The Highwaymen

Dave Fisher of New Haven was a member of a New Haven vocal harmony group called the Academics. All members of the Academics were students at New Haven's Hillhouse High School.

After graduating from Hillhouse High, Fisher attended Wesleyan University in Middletown. As a freshman at Wesleyan (fall of 1958), Fisher cofounded a folk group called the Highwaymen. The members of the Highwaymen were Dave Fisher, Bob Burnett, Steve Butts, Chan Daniels and Steve Trott.

In 1961, the Highwaymen released their mega-hit single "Michael, Row the Boat Ashore" (aka "Michael"). The song rose to the top of the *Billboard* charts and was the No. 1 song in the United States for two weeks. The song was also No. 1 in the United Kingdom and a Top 10 hit in other parts of Europe. In Connecticut, "Michael" was named the No. 1 song for the year 1961. Aside from "Michael," the Highwaymen had a No. 13 hit with "Cotton Fields." The group's other contributions to the folk scene included "The Gypsy Rover," "I'm On My Way," "Whiskey in the Jar" and "I Know Where I'm Going." In Connecticut, "The Gypsy Rover" charted in the Top 10 (No. 5 on WDRC), and "Cottonfields" charted in the Top

Dave Fisher and the Highwaymen at the Indian Neck Folk Festival, Branford, Connecticut. *Photo by Earl Colter; courtesy of the Branford Historical Society.*

20 (No. 5 on WDRC, No. 17 on WNHC). The group's self-titled LP album also charted very well in various markets, including Connecticut, where it peaked at No. 4. The group appeared on such major network shows as *The Ed Sullivan Show* and Johnny Carson's *The Tonight Show*. The Highwaymen performed many times in Connecticut, including the Indian Neck Folk Festival in Branford (May 7, 1960) and a concert at Fairfield University on August 24, 1963.

Actors Colony

The Actors Colony was located on Route 34 in Seymour, Connecticut. This music venue hosted many recording artists, well-known on a national and regional basis.

The following are some of the artists who performed at the Actors Colony:

Gene Pitney

Hall of Fame singer/songwriter Gene Pitney performed at the Actors Colony on April 10, 1965.

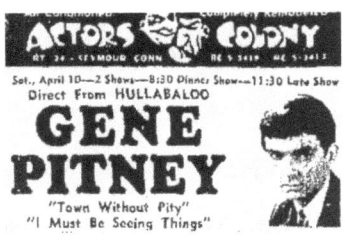

Gene Pitney at Actors Colony. *Newspapers.com.*

The Playmates

Best known for their 1958 mega-hit song "Beep Beep," the Playmates were a pop/vocal harmony trio from Waterbury, Connecticut. "Beep" was a million-seller and charted for fifteen weeks on Billboard (peaking at No. 4). The song "Beep Beep" was an extremely popular tune in Connecticut. Also, the song was a No. 1 hit in other areas of the United States (such as Buffalo's WKBW and Albany's WPTR). "Beep Beep" was also a Top 10 hit in various parts of Canada.

The popularity of "Beep Beep" helped AMC motors set production and sales records for the Rambler car models.

The group consisted of Donny Conn (born Donald Claps), Carl Cicchetti (aka Chic Hetti) and Morey Carr (aka Morey Cohen). Donny and Morey attended Waterbury's Crosby High School. They both were members of Crosby's High School Band. Chic attended Waterbury's Wilby High School. While still in high school, Chic joined Donny and Morey, forming a musical trio. Together they played local school dances and YMCA socials in the Waterbury area. After graduating from high school, the trio attended the University of Connecticut (in Storrs). While at UConn, they formed a comedy and music trio called the Nitwits and started touring in 1952. Soon after, they graduated from UConn (1953).

Other national Top 40 hits for the Playmates included "Jo-Anne," "Don't Go Home," "What Is Love" and "Wait for Me." In Connecticut, "Little Miss Stuck-Up" was a Top 10 hit (WPOP radio). The group performed at numerous music venues in Connecticut, including the Actors Colony (October 4, 1961). The Playmates disbanded in 1964.

Debbie and the Darnels

Debbie and the Darnels performed at the Actors Colony along with the Five Satins on November 27, 1962.

The Sultans

One night at Seymour's Polynesian Room we were booked with Joey Dee and the Starliters. At that time, Jimi Hendrix and Joe Pesci were a part of Joey Dee's band. They were both unknown then. Years later we found out that the Sultans had played with them. Who would believe we played with Hendrix and Pesci?! Holy Cow!

—*excerpt from* The Sultans Chronicles *by Nicholas Balzano*

We started out as four guys who loved music. Once we formed the Sultans it became a magical experience for us. We remained good friends for many, many years. All along, it was good music, great fans—and a little bit of mayhem!

—*Joe Suraci (of the Sultans)*

From the Coliseum to the Shaboo

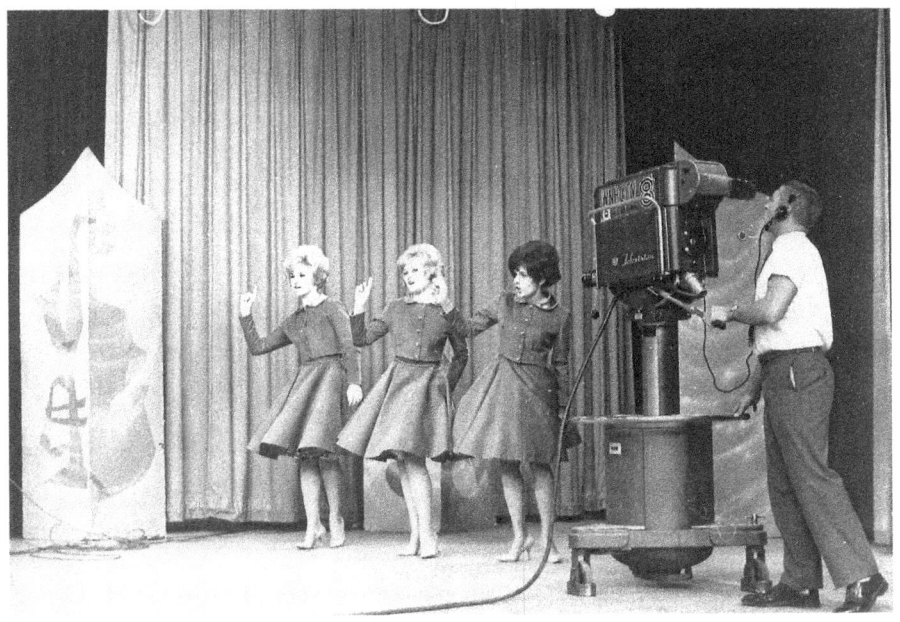

Debbie and The Darnels. *Courtesy of Dorothy Yutenkas.*

The Sultans band consisted of Joe Suraci, Larry Delucia, Paul Anastasio and Nicholas Balzano. All four band members were born in New Haven but spent most of their time in East Haven. They were all classmates at East Haven High School, graduating in 1966.

The Sultans were known for their vocals and group harmony. Their recording of "I Wanna Know" was a fan favorite and a local number one song in the greater New Haven area. The record's flip side, "Gloria," was also a popular tune in the area.

The Sultans performed in a number of Connecticut music venues, including the Actors Colony, East Haven's Dante Inferno, West Haven's House of Zodiac, Westport's Staples High School and Seymour's Polynesian Room. At one point, the group signed a two-year contract with United Artists Records and performed as the opening act for a number of well-known solo artists and bands. The group became close friends with Ginny Arnell, who also was an East Haven High School graduate. Along with a nice solo career, Ginny was part of the duo Jamie and Jane (Ginny Arnell and legendary Hall of Famer Gene Pitney).

Drummer Nicholas Balzano summed up the Sultans' experiences this way: "We had a hit record, a contract with a major recording company, a

The Sultans. *Courtesy of Nicholas Balzano.*

local number one hit, played with some of the best music artists and bands in the country and most of all we made people have fun dancing and have some good memories."

THE PROPOSED POWDER RIDGE FESTIVAL

Among the nationally known artists slated to perform at the huge Powder Ridge Festival in Middlefield, Connecticut, were legendary stars such as Janis Joplin, Sly and the Family Stone, James Taylor, Richie Havens, Fleetwood Mac, Chuck Berry, Van Morrison, Eric Burdon, Joe Cocker, Little Richard and the Allman Brothers.

However, the proposed large festival was banned and never materialized. Despite the ban, thirty thousand fans showed up in defiance.

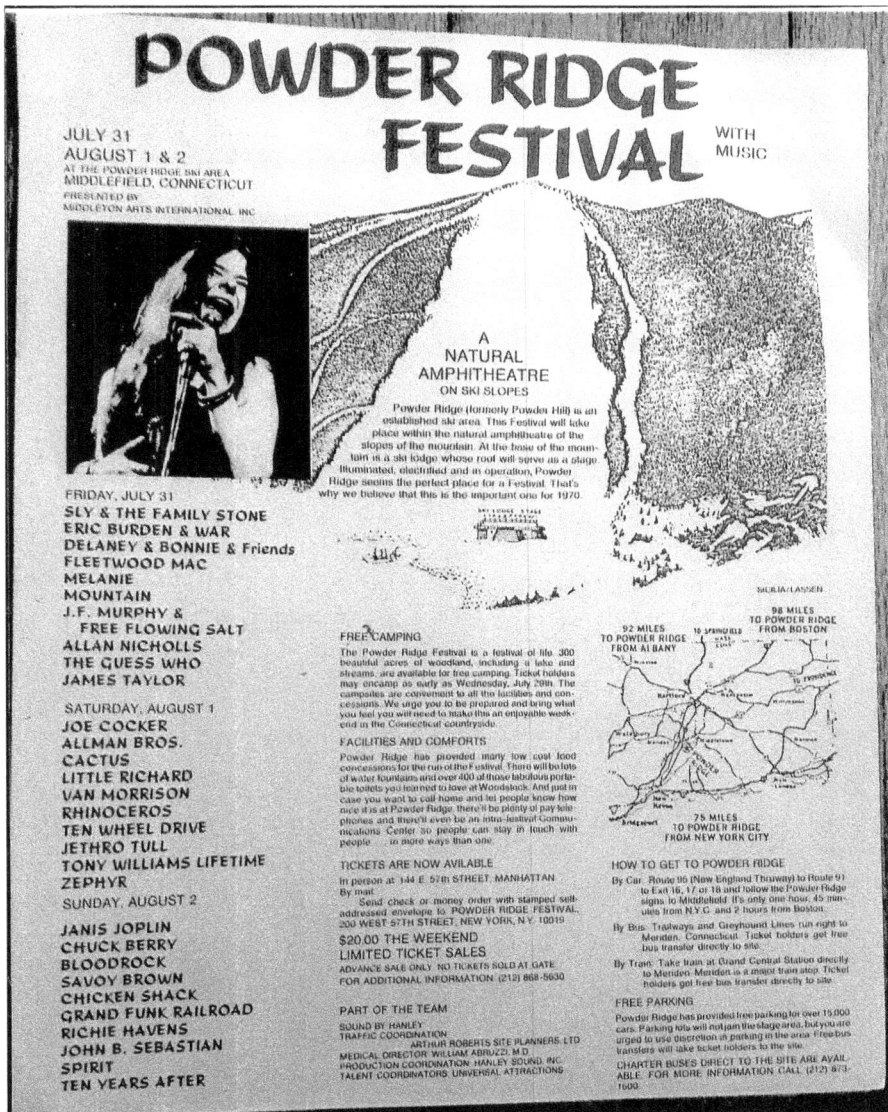

Poster of the controversial Powder Ridge Music Festival. *Author's collection.*

Historic Connecticut Music Venues

Yale Bowl ('60s and '70s)

Growing up close to the Yale Bowl, my friends and I had several ways we could sneak into the Yale Bowl. We never bought a ticket for concerts or the Yale football games. I recall seeing the Kingston Trio and also Peter, Paul and Mary in the 1960s (along with many other concerts). We would go over, under or through a fence away from suspicious eyes. We would then move around finding empty seats and move again, if necessary. We didn't attend every concert, but we could always hear the music from our neighborhood. It was a fun time for us!

—Bill Rienzi

New Haven's Yale Bowl held over seventy-five thousand fans for concerts and hosted numerous well-known national artists and bands, including Janis Joplin (July 12, 1969), the Rascals (August 2, 1969), the Eagles (with Heart and the Little River Band, June 14, 1980), Eric Clapton (June 28, 1974) and the Grateful Dead (July 31, 1971).

Yale Bowl (New Haven). *Library of Congress.*

From the Coliseum to the Shaboo

Other notable concerts at the Yale Bowl:

Led Zeppelin (Robert Plant)

Led Zeppelin performed in Connecticut on a number of occasions, including the Yale Bowl (August 15, 1970, and September 15, 1970) and the Oakdale Theatre on August 17, 1969.

Robert Plant of Led Zeppelin has performed as a soloist in various Connecticut music venues, including the Hartford Civic, New Haven Coliseum (twice), Mohegan Sun Arena (twice) and Foxwoods Theatre. Led Zeppelin was inducted into the Rock 'n' Roll Hall of Fame in 1995.

Robert Plant. *Copyright Philamonjaro.*

Paul Simon

Singer-songwriter Paul Simon and his fellow Rock 'n' Roll Hall of Fame partner Art Garfunkel performed at the Yale Bowl on August 5, 1967.

Simon and his wife, singer Edie Brickell, moved into their house in Connecticut in 2002. Prior to moving to Connecticut, Simon was familiar with the state, having performed in Connecticut on numerous occasions.

Paul Simon, as a solo performer, coheadlined a concert with Bob Dylan on July 24, 1999, at The Meadows Music Theatre. Simon has performed in a number of other Connecticut music venues, including Mohegan Sun (three times), Foxwoods, Meadows Music Theatre (three times), the Hartford Civic Center and Fairfield University with Art Garfunkel (September 10, 1966).

During the time he has lived in Connecticut, Simon has recorded six singles and two albums. Simon's album *So Beautiful or So What* (2011) was recorded in Connecticut at Simon's house. Edie Brickell provided some of the backup vocals. The album was well received by music critics, ranking No. 4 on U.S. *Billboard*, No. 6 on UK charts and No. 7 in Canada. Simon's previous album, *Surprise* (2006), was ranked No. 14 on *Billboard* and No. 4 in the United Kingdom. On April 28, 2016, Paul Simon released "Cool Papa Bell" from his album *Stranger to Stranger*. His latest album, *In the Blue Light*, was released in September 2018.

Yale Bowl Notes

- Purportedly, the Yale Bowl turned down a request by the Beatles to perform at the Bowl in August 1964, the year that the Beatles arrived in America. It has been reported that a wealthy Yale donor threatened to withdraw his donation to the medical school if the Beatles played at the Yale Bowl.
- In 1990, Paul McCartney was not allowed to perform at Yale Bowl due to neighborhood opposition.

Heart

Heart, including sisters Ann and Nancy Wilson, performed at the Yale Bowl on June 14, 1980. The band also played at Mohegan Sun (six times), New Haven Coliseum (three times), Foxwoods (six times), The Meadows, Oakdale and Hartford Civic Center (two times). Heart was inducted into the Rock 'n' Roll Hall of Fame in 2013.

Heart, with Ann (*right*) and Nancy Wilson. *Copyright Ivor Levene.*

From the Coliseum to the Shaboo

QUIGLEY STADIUM

In August 1961, Quigley Stadium was the site of a blockbuster oldies show. The headliners were the Isley Brothers and included many notable acts such as Jimmy "Handyman" Jones, the Fiestas, the Shells, the Kodacs and the Hearts. Representing Connecticut were the Nutmegs and our group Roger Koob and the Premiers. Backing all of these acts was the Alan Freed Band with Sam "The Man" Taylor, Big Al Sears and Panama Francis.

Since this was a baseball stadium, the stage was set up in the vicinity of the pitcher's mound. A huge tent was erected over second base and was a place for everyone to gather and was used as a universal dressing room. When the Isley Brothers arrived in the tent, they were easily recognizable, especially Ronnie Isley. He wore a bright reddish maroon short-sleeved shirt. To everyone's surprise, the two brothers were low key and quiet prior to going on stage.

It was a hot August day, and the huge crowd was about to be treated to one helluva show. The Premiers opened the show, followed by Jimmy Jones who performed his hits "Handyman" and "Good Timing." The Shells then came on stage wearing their yellow suits with black lapels and stripes down their legs. They then proceeded to go into a series of splits, which captivated the crowd.

When the Isley Brothers took the stage, everyone was out of their seats, waiting in anticipation. The Isley Brothers did not disappoint. When the group began their song "Shout," some of the kids jumped onto the dugouts, which were located near the stage. Ronnie Isley began to leave the stage and [walk] out toward the stands. The crowd was beginning to show signs of getting out of control. Suddenly, Ronnie took off his red jacket and started to act as a toreador at a bull fight, taunting the crowd as a bull fighter would taunt a bull. Suddenly all hell broke loose as the crowd jumped over the dugouts and onto the field. The Isley Brothers dropped their mikes and ran toward the tent. It was like a tsunami as the crowd came in a wave across the field. Music sheets were flying all over the place, and music stands crumpled over in the fury. It was a wild scene. Although the police were not able to control the crowd, they were able to provide enough security around the tent to ensure safety. It wasn't a violent crowd, just an excited one. There were no injuries. It was just an explosive ending to a great concert.

—Bill Koob, of the Premiers

West Haven's Quigley Stadium was the site of two chaotic but nonviolent concerts. As noted in the quote from Bill Koob, the police were overwhelmed by the large number of fans who rushed the stage in response to the Isley Brothers and their fun antics during their performance at Quigley in August 1961.

Eight years later, a similar incident took place when Sly and the Family Stone performed at Quigley Stadium. The legendary group took the stage at Quigley on August 12, 1969. As Sly began to sing, the crowd got out of control and rushed the stage and created chaos on the field. Like the reaction to the Isley Brothers at Quigley, the crowd for Sly and the Family Stone was not violent but rather excited and energized.

The Premiers

Roger Koob and the Premiers performed at Quigley Stadium. *Left to right:* Gus Delcos, Frankie Pelomus, Billy Koob and Roger Koob. *Courtesy of Bill Koob.*

From the Coliseum to the Shaboo

Hartford Civic Center. *Author's collection.*

Hartford Civic Center

> *Connecticut music venues, like those throughout the U.S., serve as a place where fans gather together to hear great music performed live by their favorite bands. It's where the musician can feel the energy of the audience and where the artist's music comes to life.*
> —Ray Lamitola, of South Michigan Avenue

The Hartford Civic Center (now known as the XL Center) is located in downtown Hartford.

The following are some of the artists who performed at the Hartford Civic Center:

Elvis Presley

Elvis Presley was scheduled to perform in concert at the Hartford Civic Center on August 21, 1977. However, he passed away just five days before

Historic Connecticut Music Venues

on Tuesday afternoon, August 16, 1977. He did perform at the Hartford Civic Center on July 28, 1976. Elvis Presley was one of the first inductees into the Rock 'n' Roll Hall of Fame in 1986. Presley has been inducted into numerous other music Halls of Fame.

Paul McCartney

Paul McCartney performed in concert at the Hartford Civic Center on September 27, 2002, as part of his "Back in the U.S." tour. McCartney was inducted by Mick Jagger into the Rock 'n' Roll Hall of Fame as a member of the Beatles in 1988. Paul McCartney was again inducted into the Hall of Fame (by Neil Young) as a solo artist in 1999.

The Rolling Stones

The legendary Hall of Fame band the Rolling Stones performed in concert at the Hartford Civic Center on five occasions. The Stones also performed at Toad's Place, East Hartford's Rentschler Field, Dillon Stadium and the New Haven Arena.

Top: Elvis Presley passed away days before his scheduled 1977 appearance at the Hartford Civic Center. *Author's collection.*

Middle: Paul and Linda McCartney. Charles Rosenay, Stacey Eisenberg. Liverpool Tours. *Courtesy of Charles Rosenay, producer.*

Bottom: DJ Dick Robinson interviewing the Rolling Stones (at the WDRC studio) prior to their performance in Hartford. *Courtesy of Robinson Entertainment, LLC.*

Ricky Nelson

Ricky Nelson performed at the Hartford Civic Center on November 19, 1983. On New Year's Eve, December 31, 1985, Nelson perished in a plane crash while heading for a concert in Dallas, Texas. He was forty-five years old. Ricky Nelson was inducted into the Rock 'n' Roll Hall of Fame in 1987.

Meat Loaf

Meat Loaf. *Courtesy of Anastasia Pantsios.*

Meat Loaf, one of the bestselling music artists of all time, lived in Connecticut's Fairfield County for nearly ten years, from 1979 to end of 1988. During that time, the singer released five albums and twenty-one singles and had six major tours. Also, during this period, Meat Loaf appeared in six feature films and was involved in three TV shows (including an *SNL* musical guest appearance).

Meat Loaf is the stage name of Michael Lee Aday (born Marvin Lee Aday). He is probably best known for his exceptional album trilogy *Bat Out of Hell*, consisting of *Bat Out of Hell*, *Bat Out of Hell II: Back into Hell* and *Bat Out of Hell III: The Monster Is Loose*.

Meat Loaf's recordings charted well on Connecticut radio charts, especially "Two Out of Three Ain't Bad," which was a No. 1 hit in Connecticut (WAVZ). Meat Loaf appeared at a number of music venues in Connecticut, including the Hartford Civic Center, the Mohegan Sun (six times), The Meadows Music Theatre, Toad's Place (twice) and Pinecrest Country Club.

Bruce Springsteen

Bruce Springsteen performed at the Hartford Civic Center on eight occasions.

Bruce Springsteen. *Copyright Ivor Levene.*

Gary Burr

Gary Burr was born and raised in Meriden and graduated from Platt High School. Burr is an extremely successful singer-songwriter. In 1982, Burr's "Love's Been a Little Bit Hard on Me" was a No. 7 *Billboard* hit song for Juice Newton. The song was also a Top 10 hit on Connecticut radio stations (No. 6 on WDRC). He has written songs that became hits for many major country recording artists such as Reba McEntire, Kenny Rogers, Tim McGraw, Garth Brooks, Randy Travis, Kelly Clarkson, Faith Hill and others.

Gary has received over twenty American Society of Composers, Authors and Publishers (ASCAP) awards. He was ASCAP's Country Songwriter of the Year in 1995. Burr was also named Songwriter of the Year by the Nashville Songwriters Association (NSAI) in 1992 and 1994.

Gary Burr was a member of the group Pure Prairie League for several years and has also recorded as a solo artist. Pure Prairie League performed at the Hartford Civic Center on December 26, 1977.

Burr is currently a member of Blue Sky Riders, featuring Burr, Kenny Loggins and Burr's wife (and fellow songwriter), Georgia Middleman. In 2014, Gary Burr was inducted into the Meriden Hall of Fame.

Billy Joel (and also Elton John)

Billy Joel performed at the Hartford Civic Center on at least nineteen occasions. Also, Billy Joel and Elton John shared the stage at the Hartford Civic Center on four occasions in February 2002.

Eric Clapton

Eric Clapton. *Copyright Philamonjaro.*

Three-time Rock 'n' Roll Hall of Fame inductee Eric Clapton performed at the Hartford Civic Center on six occasions. Clapton was inducted as a solo artist on March 6, 2000. Eric Clapton was previously inducted to the Hall of Fame as a member of Cream in 1993 and as a member of the Yardbirds in 1992.

From the Coliseum to the Shaboo

The American Shakespeare Theatre. *Courtesy of the Newman S. Hungerford Museum Fund, CHS.*

AMERICAN SHAKESPEARE THEATRE (STRATFORD)

The American Shakespeare Festival Theatre (AST) opened on July 12, 1955, with a performance of *Julius Caesar*. The theater closed in 1989 and burned to the ground on January 13, 2019.

During the 1970s and mid-1980s, AST hosted numerous major recording artists, including the Kinks (twice), Cat Stevens, Gordon Lightfoot, Badfinger, Taj Mahal, Don McLean, Jackson Browne, the Four Tops, the Temptations and Roberta Flack.

Other notable performances at the American Shakespeare Theatre:

Neil Young's Live Recording at American Shakespeare Theatre

On January 22, 1971, Neil Young recorded his live album *Young Shakespeare* at Stratford's American Shakespeare Theatre. The album sat idle for fifty years until it was finally released on March 26, 2021.

Filmed by a European television crew, the video of this live performance at the Shakespeare Theatre is believed to be one of the oldest known films of a Neil Young solo concert.

Laura Nyro

On my Destiny *album, the song "Love Came" was very important to me because Laura Nyro was my guest artist on that song. Laura was simply phenomenal. Man, she was so good and a very dear friend. She and I both lived in Danbury for a good deal of time. I was so blessed to have the opportunity to record with her and to have known Laura Nyro.*
—Felix Cavaliere

Singer, songwriter and pianist Laura Nyro lived on Zinn Road in Danbury, Connecticut, for twenty-two years. On April 8, 1997, Laura passed away at her home in Danbury. She was only forty-nine years old. Laura's ashes were buried underneath a Japanese maple tree planted by her friends outside her bedroom window at her Danbury cottage.

Laura Nyro performed at the American Shakespeare Theatre on September 13, 1972, and September 15, 1972. Laura also performed at the New Haven Arena, Bushnell Memorial (twice), Oakdale Theatre and Toad's Place.

Nyro achieved fame as a songwriter with major hits: "Eli's Coming" (Three Dog Night), "And When I Die" (Blood Sweat and Tears/Peter, Paul and Mary), "Stoney End" (Barbra Streisand), and the Fifth Dimension's "Wedding Bell Blues" and "Stoned Soul Picnic."

Laura released a number of albums and singles herself, most notably Carole King's "Up on the Roof" (the live version of this song appears on her 2002 reissued album *Gonna Take a Miracle*).

Nyro has been praised for her soulful and emotional singing style and has influenced countless recording artists.

Laura Nyro was posthumously inducted into the Rock 'n' Roll Hall of Fame in 2012, the Songwriters Hall of Fame in 2010 and the Connecticut Women's Hall of Fame in 2001.

Laura Nyro. *Author's collection.*

From the Coliseum to the Shaboo

DILLON STADIUM

In a live environment, the more bodies you put in a room, the more energy there will be. That's a real big payoff. That's really important, the live show, it's a big cycle of energy.
—*attributed to James Lee Lindsey Jr.*

My dad was Charlie Parker, disc jockey at WDRC. So, I spent most of my early years backstage with my dad at all the WDRC/Big D shows. As a teenager I worked for a couple of years with Jimmy Koplick (a good friend) at Dillon stadium. Some of the wildest and biggest rock acts I have ever seen! I am so blessed because, as Charlie's son, I got to personally meet famous performers as Jimi Hendrix, Janis Joplin, the Four Seasons, the Beach Boys, the Rolling Stones, Bobby Rydell, the Supremes, Elton John and many more.
   I loved all the rock concerts at Connecticut music venues!
—Steve Parker

Fans flock to Dillon Stadium for the Grateful Dead concert, July 31, 1974. *Copyright 1974 James R. Anderson.*

Historic Connecticut Music Venues

Charlie Watts of the Rolling Stones. *Copyright Ivor Levene.*

Hartford's Dillon Stadium was built in 1935, and during its long history, this large venue has played host to many concerts featuring nationally known artists and bands. On July 31, 1974, the Grateful Dead recorded their performance at Dillon Stadium, and the live album titled *Dave's Picks Volume 2* was subsequently released on May 1, 2012. Other notable groups that performed at Dillon Stadium include Faces, the Beach Boys, the Allman Brothers, the Rolling Stones, the Doors, the Kinks, Jefferson Airplane and Santana. At this time, the stadium is the home of the USL Hartford Athletic professional soccer team.

Rod Stewart (Faces)

On July 10, 1972, Rod Stewart performed at Dillon Stadium as a member of the Hall of Fame band Faces. Previously, Stewart was a member of the Jeff Beck group. Both Rod Stewart and Jeff Beck are in the select group of artists who were inducted into the Rock 'n' Roll Hall of Fame twice. Stewart entered the Hall of Fame as a member of Faces and as a solo artist (when he was inducted by Jeff Beck). Likewise, Jeff Beck was inducted into the Hall of Fame on two occasions (the Yardbirds and as a solo artist).

Rod Stewart and Jeff Beck. *Copyright Ivor Levene.*

2
MUSIC VENUES—PRESENT

Music venues are places for fans to meet up, listen to some great live music, dance a little and just have a whole lot of fun!
—Al Anderson of the Wildweeds and NRBQ

CAFE 9 (AKA CAFE NINE)

New Haven's "tiny but mighty" Cafe Nine has long been the jewel in the crown of Connecticut's original music venues. Seven nights a week, fifty-two weeks a year, the owners—first, Mike Reichbart, and now, for many years, Paul Mayer— have committed to presenting local and national touring acts whose bread and butter comes from the songs they, themselves, write. I'm proud to be included in this stellar bunch and have premiered all six of my CDs at the Nine. Those in the know in Connecticut know...Cafe Nine is the hippest, and the coolest!
—Christine Ohlman

Cafe 9 (aka Cafe Nine) is a popular and much-loved music venue. Over the years, Cafe Nine has hosted numerous well-known national and regional artists and bands.

HISTORIC CONNECTICUT MUSIC VENUES

Entrance to the Cafe Nine music venue. *Copyright Tom Kaszuba.*

The following are some of the artists who performed at Cafe Nine:

Al Anderson (of the Wildweeds, NRBQ, solo career)

Big Al Anderson is the mack daddy of the Connecticut original music scene. He's the king…forever.

—Christine Ohlman

Singer-songwriter-guitarist Al Anderson (aka "Big Al") was born and raised in Windsor, Connecticut. Anderson's band experience began at age eleven with the Connecticut band the Visuals, followed by the high school bands the Altones, the Blues Messengers and the Six Packs. In 1966, the Six Packs were renamed the Wildweeds. Thanks to Anderson's distinctive lead vocals and great song lyrics, the Wildweeds remain one of Connecticut's most well-known and revered bands.

Having departed the Wildweeds, Big Al's next venture was joining the New Rhythm and Blues Quartet (NRBQ) at the end of 1971. He was a member of NRBQ from 1971 until 1993. Anderson's first major songwriting and vocal contribution to this group was the fan-favorite 1977

NRBQ song "Ridin' in My Car." The song became an instant classic and a staple at NRBQ concerts. Even during his stint with NRBQ, Anderson pursued a well-received solo career, beginning with the 1972 self-titled LP *Al Anderson*. The album was a Top 10 hit in Connecticut (No. 8 on Hartford's WDRC). He has recorded a number of solo albums since.

In 1993, Anderson wrote a tune called "Every Little Thing" that was recorded by Carlene Carter (daughter of June Carter). The song (cowritten by Carlene) became a smash hit, reaching No. 3 on the country charts. After spending over twenty years with NRBQ, Anderson decided to leave the group and concentrate most of his time and energy as a songwriter. Big Al is considered one of the most prolific songwriters in the music industry. Besides songs written during his Wildweeds and NRBQ days, Anderson's songwriting achievements resulted in hits for major artists, including Vince Gill, Tim McGraw, Trisha Yearwood, Jimmy Buffett, Bonnie Raitt, Alabama, the Oak Ridge Boys, George Jones, LeAnn Rimes and George Strait.

Al Anderson has performed in many Connecticut music venues as a member of the Wildweeds, NRBQ and a solo artist. As a soloist, Anderson has played at Cafe Nine and Old Saybrook's The Kate (among others). As a member of the Wildweeds, Al performed with the band at venues such as the Shack and the Cheri Shack. Al Anderson played with NRBQ at many Connecticut music venues, including the Shaboo Inn (nearly thirty times), Toad's Place (over ten times), the Agora (four times), Storrs' UCONN (six times), New Britain's the Sting (three times), New Haven Arena, Players Tavern, Pinecrest Country Club, Waterbury's City Limits, Wesleyan University, Milford's Foran High School, Waterbury's Library Park and Levitt Pavilion.

Among his many accolades, in 1993, Anderson was voted one of the top one hundred guitarists of the twentieth century by *Musician Magazine*. In 2000, Anderson was named BMI Songwriter of the Year. Al Anderson is a gifted singer, songwriter and guitarist and truly one of Connecticut's music gems.

Al Anderson performing at Cafe Nine. *Copyright Tom Kaszuba.*

Historic Connecticut Music Venues

Christine Ohlman, the "Beehive Queen"

Singer, songwriter and guitarist Christine Ohlman has called Connecticut her home for many years, having moved from the Bronx to Meriden and finally to Cheshire. She attended Notre Dame Academy in Waterbury. Her brother, Vic Steffens, went to Cheshire Academy. Nicknamed the "Beehive Queen," Ohlman has been involved in a number of bands and projects in her career. Her music genres are mainly soul, R&B and rock 'n' roll.

Christine recalled growing up with a love of music:

> *I have been singing for as long as I can remember. When I was little, I would constantly put on shows for the family, sometimes with my cousin. I remember standing in front of the mirror singing when I was just a little kid. I was always singing around the house and when I was in school. My parents couldn't shut me up! This was probably the reason why I got involved in a band in the first place.*

When she was only sixteen years old, Ohlman, then a high school student, joined a New Haven blues/rock band called the Wrongh Black Bag. Ohlman was the band's lead singer, and her younger brother, Vic, was the group's drummer. When she was a high school senior, the band recorded "Wake Me Shake Me," which charted on *Billboard*. The song appears on a compilation album called *Psychedelic Archaeology*. The flip side was "I Don't Know Why," which was released on a great compilation album called *All Kind of Highs* in 2012 that features psych/rock songs. The Wrongh Black Bag opened for the Wildweeds, and Christine and Al Anderson have been close friends ever since then.

Christine and Vic's next band was called Fancy. They released an LP album, *Fancy Meeting You Here*, and a 45rpm record "All My Best." The band recorded at Thomas "Doc" Cavalier's Trod Nossel Studios (formerly Syncron). Later, Steffens joined the Connecticut band Napi Browne. He also formed his own recording studio.

Once Fancy disbanded, Ohlman became a member of the Scratch Band, which was popular in the Northeast, most notably for live performances. Christine has always felt that the Scratch Band was way ahead of its time. This is the reason, Christine feels, that each of the members of the Scratch Band went on to achieve success in the music business. The Scratch Band featured such talented musicians as G.E. Smith, Robert Orsi, Paul Ossola, Mickey Curry, Bill Durso and Ray Zeiner. Guitarist G.E. Smith performed with notable artists such as Hall & Oates and eventually became the musical director of the *Saturday Night Live* TV show. Curry has worked with a number of major stars, including Hall & Oates, Bryan Adams, David Bowie, the Cult and Alice Cooper. Zeiner became a member of the popular Wildweeds band. After the Scratch Band, Ohlman founded the group Christine Ohlman and the Soul Rockers.

In 1991, Ohlman reunited with G.E. Smith when she joined the Saturday Night Live Band as the lead singer, and she is still with SNL.

Ohlman is currently the lead singer of Christine Ohlman and Rebel Montez. Christine has recorded six CDs with Rebel Montez and toured throughout the Northeast with the band. She has also performed with several other bands, including an all-star band at Cleveland's Rock 'n' Roll Hall of Fame, the NYC Hit Squad and the Decoys, in Muscle Shoals, Alabama.

Two of the studios in which Ohlman has recorded her music are located in Connecticut. One studio belongs to her brother, Vic Steffens (West Haven's Horizon Music Group). The other studio belonged to her longtime mate "Doc" Cavalier (Trod Nossel Studios in Wallingford). Ohlman has been backed up by the fabulous Sin Sisters (Kathy Kessler, Janice Ingarra and Patti Rahl) when performing in Connecticut shoreline towns.

As noted, Christine Ohlman, as a member of the Wrongh Black Bag, opened for the Wildweeds early in her career. Things came full circle when Christine performed with a reunited Wildweeds band in their 2011, 2014

Christine Ohlman with Rebel Montez and the Sin Sisters. *Courtesy of Tom Horan.*

and 2015 concerts. She sang the harmony parts of the Wildweeds' bassist Bob Dudek.

Christine has performed at Cafe 9 along with her friend Al Anderson. She has also performed in numerous other Connecticut music venues with her band Rebel Montez, including Toad's Place, Black Eyed Sally's, the Kate, Comcast Theatre and Fairfield Theatre Company.

Christine Ohlman is an iconic musical artist and performer, especially in the Northeast and her two "second musical homes" in New Orleans and Muscle Shoals. Famed music critic Dave Marsh has labeled Christine's music as "contemporary rock R&B."

Christine summed up her career as follows: "Whatever I am and whatever I have become as a musician is the sum total of all the different music influences that I have absorbed in my life."

The Reducers

The Reducers were a long-running rock band from New London, Connecticut. The band formed in 1978, inspired by the English punk rock movement of the time. The four band members were Hugh Birdsall (guitar, vocals), Peter Detmold (guitar, vocals), Steve Kaika (bass, vocals) and Tom Trombley (drums, vocals). The Reducers released many LPs, CDs and 45s on their own Rave On record label, beginning with 1980s double A-side single "Out of Step"/"No Ambition." Ken Evans (of the Fifth Estate) was the manager of the Reducers in the 1980s.

Roger C. Reale collaborated with the Reducers on a three-song EP titled *Wake the Neighbors*, which was recorded in 1987. In 1977, Reale released the cult classic *Radioactive* LP album on Doc Cavalier's Big Sound record label. The album was recorded at Cavalier's Trod Nossel Studios. A longtime presence on the Connecticut music scene, Roger has also performed and recorded with the Manchurians.

The Reducers performed at a number of music venues in Connecticut, including Cafe Nine and the Shaboo Inn. The Reducers remained active for thirty-four years, inspiring a loyal, cult-like fan following.

The Reducers. *Used with permission from the Reducers, and Ken Evans.*

From the Coliseum to the Shaboo

Bouchard Brothers, formerly of Blue Öyster Cult, at Cafe Nine. *Copyright Nora Kaszuba.*

OAKDALE THEATRE

The biggest entertainers make Oakdale a "must."
—*Oakdale website*

I spent many wonderful times watching my dad perform at Oakdale Theatre.
—*Bonnie Raitt*

The Oakdale Theatre was built in 1954. The original Oakdale, founded by Ben Segal, was actually built as a theatre-in-the-round complete with a revolving stage and a large tent protecting a seating capacity of 1,700. In 1972, a wood dome was erected, and the seating capacity was increased to 3,200. In 1996, the Oakdale was completely renovated, transforming the old theatre-in-the-round into a large auditorium-style venue with a seating capacity of 4,800, with an additional 1,600 seats available at Oakdale's Dome theatre. Oakdale became part of Live Nation when it joined with the legendary Connecticut promoter Jim Koplik.

The Oakdale Theatre has undergone a number of name changes throughout the years, including the Oakdale Musical Theatre, SNET Oakdale Theatre, ctnow.com Oakdale Theatre, careerbuilder.com Oakdale Theatre, Chevrolet Theatre and Toyota Oakdale Theatre. Despite these name changes, most people refer to this music venue simply as the Oakdale Theatre.

For over sixty years, the Oakdale Theatre has been an extremely popular music venue in the region, attracting major national performers.

Oakdale Theatre. *Author's collection.*

The following are some of the artists who have performed at the Oakdale Theatre:

Felix Cavaliere

> *Felix Cavaliere is an iconic musician who does it all—singer, songwriter, keyboard player—you name it. And that amazing voice! The Rascals were outstanding. I'm so glad I had the chance to record and perform in concerts with Felix on and off for a number of years.*
> —Scott Spray, Grammy recording bassist

Felix Cavaliere lived in Danbury for over seventeen years (from 1969 to late 1986). During the period he lived in Connecticut, Cavaliere recorded at least five albums and eleven singles with his legendary band the Rascals before the group's breakup in 1972. Also while living in Danbury, Cavaliere recorded and released at least four solo albums. In 1980, his solo recording "Only a Lonely Heart Sees" was a Top 40 hit on *Billboard* (No. 36), a No. 2 hit on the Adult Contemporary chart and a Top 20 song on local Connecticut radio stations (No. 14).

Prior to moving to Connecticut, Cavaliere was familiar with this state, having performed in Connecticut on several occasions with the Young Rascals, including concerts at the New Haven Arena on Saturday, May 7, 1966, and at Westport's Staples High School on February 19, 1967.

In 2013, Cavaliere reunited with his original Rascals bandmates (Eddie Brigati, Dino Danelli and Gene Cornish) and appeared on Broadway in their production of *Once Upon a Dream*.

As a soloist, Felix Cavaliere performed at the Oakdale (Chevrolet Theatre) on July 27, 2007. Felix and the artists he has performed with have played in numerous other music venues in Connecticut, including the Shaboo Inn (December 1, 1977) and Meadows Music Theatre and as a member of Ringo Starr & His All-Starr Band.

Felix just finished writing his memoir, titled *The King of Blue Eyed Soul*. He also recently released a new CD called *Then and Now* featuring songs that influenced him as a musician as well as five original songs written by Felix. For more information about his book and CD, visit www.felixcavalieremusic.com.

Felix Cavaliere has been inducted into the Rock 'n' Roll Hall of Fame (with the Rascals), the Songwriter's Hall of Fame (2009), Vocal Group Hall of Fame (with the Rascals) and Grammy Hall of Fame (with the Rascals).

As noted earlier, Felix Cavaliere and his band the Rascals recorded a number of hit records during Cavaliere's residence in Connecticut (1969–86). To give you an idea of how some of these recordings fared on Connecticut radio surveys versus how the songs charted on *Billboard*, here are comparisons:

- "A Ray of Hope" | *Billboard* ranking No. 24, Connecticut peak position No. 2.
- "Heaven" | *Billboard* ranking No. 39, Connecticut peak position No. 3.
- "See" | *Billboard* ranking No. 27, Connecticut peak position No. 7.
- "Carry Me Back" | *Billboard* ranking No. 26, Connecticut peak position No. 3.
- "Hold On" | *Billboard* ranking No. 51, Connecticut peak position No. 14.
- "Glory" | *Billboard* ranking No. 58, Connecticut peak position No. 28.
- Solo hit recording by Felix Cavaliere, "Only the Lonely Heart Sees" | *Billboard* ranking No. 36, Connecticut peak position No. 14.

HISTORIC CONNECTICUT MUSIC VENUES

The Doors and the Wildweeds Concert at Oakdale

The Wildweeds shared the stage with Jim Morrison and the Doors for two sold-out concerts at the Oakdale Theatre on September 23–24, 1967.

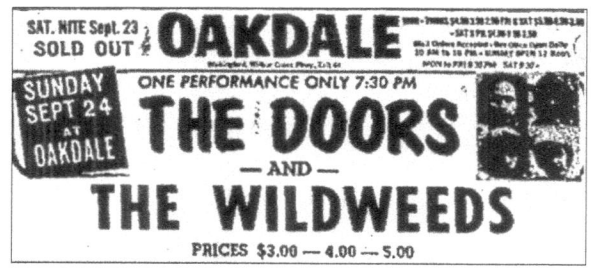

The Wildweeds and Doors ad at the Oakdale Theatre. *Author's collection.*

The Carpenters

Karen Carpenter has the best female voice in the world: melodic, tuneful and distinctive.

—*Paul McCartney*

Both Karen and Richard Carpenter were born and raised in New Haven, Connecticut. The siblings were born at Grace–New Haven Hospital (renamed Yale–New Haven Hospital). Their father, Harold Bertram Carpenter, worked for the New Haven Pulp and Board Company. Their mother, Agnes, was a housewife. While in school, Agnes enjoyed playing various sports, with a keen interest in basketball and baseball. Harold and Agnes moved to New Haven in 1940, and the Carpenter family lived on Hall Street.

Richard attended Nathan Hale Elementary School (Townsend Avenue), which was right around the block from the Carpenters' home on Hall Street. He played music at a very early age, first the accordion (at age four) and then piano (at age eight). Richard attended Wilbur Cross High School, where he displayed his musical talent. When he was fifteen years old, he studied piano at Yale Music School. At this same time, Richard formed his own group consisting of piano, bass and drums, and the trio played at local venues in and around New Haven. At age sixteen, Richard made his recording debut when he joined the Barries for their songs "Why Don't You Write Me" and "Mary Ann." Richard played the piano on these recordings.

Karen and Richard Carpenter in front of their house on Hall Street, New Haven. *Courtesy of Randy L. Schmidt, author.*

Karen also attended Nathan Hale Elementary School. Unlike Richard, her concentration was on activities other than music. Just like her mother, Karen enjoyed playing sports, especially baseball. Along with her friends, Karen would participate in baseball games on the street in front of her Hall Street house or at New Haven's Nathan Hale Park. In the book *Little Girl Blue*, author Randy L. Schmidt writes, "A favorite was Wiffleball, a variation on baseball that used a perforated plastic ball invented just thirty miles away by a man in Fairfield. Karen pitched and sometimes played first base. 'I was a tremendous baseball fan,' she later said. 'I memorized all the batting averages long before I knew the first word to a song. The Yankees were my favorites.'" Karen also had a paper route; she delivered the *New Haven Register* newspaper on a daily basis. Karen and Richard's elementary school (Nathan Hale School) honored Richard and Karen Carpenter with the school's Hall of Fame Award.

In the summer of 1963, the Carpenters moved to Downey, California. Karen and Richard, of course, went on to become one of the bestselling recording artists of all time with their group the Carpenters, selling a staggering number of records (well over 100 million) worldwide, including three No. 1 singles, five No. 2 singles and twelve Top 10 singles. They were the premier music act of the 1970s.

The Carpenters' songs resonated with Connecticut residents and were consistently played on local radio stations. Their songs reached the Top 10 and even No. 1 on popular Connecticut radio stations, such as WAVZ, WNHC, WPOP and WDRC.

In Connecticut, the Carpenters performed at the Oakdale Theatre on six occasions in 1973 (July 10–July 15, 1973).

Note: There is a connection between New Haven's Karen and Richard Carpenter and Windsor's Al Anderson. When he was with the Wildweeds, Al Anderson wrote and recorded the song "And When She Smiles." The Carpenters (with Karen as the lead singer) performed this song at their concerts. Previously unreleased, the tune was finally released (with the title changed to "And When He Smiles") in 2004 on the CD titled *As Time Goes By*.

HISTORIC CONNECTICUT MUSIC VENUES

Herman's Hermits

The Herman's Hermits performed at Oakdale Theatre on August 11, 1968.

Gordon Lightfoot

The legendary Gordon Lightfoot performed at the Oakdale Theatre on June 20, 1982, August 1, 1985, August 20, 1987, July 25, 1991, and August 1, 1993.

The Who

The Who performed at the Oakdale Theatre on July 21, 1968. The Who were inducted into the Rock 'n' Roll Hall of Fame in 1990.

Brian Wilson

Brian Wilson performed *Pet Sounds* in its entirety to celebrate the fiftieth anniversary of the legendary album on September 27, 2016. Brian played at Oakdale on five other occasions.

Top: Herman's Hermits at Oakdale (with fan in front). *Courtesy of Henry McNulty.*

Middle: Gordon Lightfoot backstage at the Oakdale Theatre signing autographs for author's family (1991). *Author's collection.*

Bottom: Members of The Who backstage in the Oakdale Theatre dressing room. *Courtesy of Henry McNulty.*

From the Coliseum to the Shaboo

Led Zeppelin

Led Zeppelin performed at Oakdale on August 17, 1969.

Bonnie Raitt

Bonnie Raitt played at Oakdale on August 12, 2016. Note: Bonnie Raitt's musical talent is in her DNA, as her father (John Raitt) was a veteran of Oakdale's theatre-in-the-round, having performed in quite a few major musicals in the 1960s at Oakdale, including *Oklahoma!*, *Carousel* and *Pajama Game*, among others. He was considered at the time to be the most popular male vocalist at Oakdale.

Alicia Keys

Alicia Keys's very first show of her initial concert tour was at the Oakdale Theatre on January 22, 2001.

Edgar Winter

Edgar Winter performed at Oakdale with Rick Derringer (who once lived in Colchester).

MGMT

During their freshman year (2002) at Middletown's Wesleyan University, Ben Goldwasser and Andrew VanWyngarden formed the psychedelic/indie rock band Management, later changed to MGMT. In a short period of time, MGMT has released an impressive number of well-received singles, EPs and albums to an international audience. The band's 2007 debut album, *Oracular Spectacular*, charted in the Top 40 in the United States and Top 10 in Europe. The album achieved gold record status in the United States and platinum in Europe. MGMT has received numerous major award nominations, including Grammy nominations, and has an extremely loyal international fan base.

MGMT has performed in a number of Connecticut music venues, including Oakdale and New Haven's College Street Music Hall (formerly the New Haven Palace Theatre).

The Bram Rigg Set

The Bram Rigg Set were the opening act for the Dave Clark Five at the Oakdale Theatre on July 9, 1967.

Connecticut's Bram Rigg Set (BRS) was a garage rock band with a loyal local following. BRS's Beau Segal and Bobby Schlosser were previously in a band called George's Boys. "I Can Only Give You Everything" by BRS charted locally and appeared in other markets, such as Columbus (Ohio) and Providence. The tune also appeared as a "bubbling under" song on *Billboard*'s Hot 100. The band recorded at "Doc" Cavalier's Syncron Studios (later named Trod Nossel Studio) in Wallingford.

BRS songs appear on a compilation album titled *Don't Press Your Luck! The IN Sound of 60s Connecticut* (2008), which features a number of great rock and garage rock bands from Connecticut. BRS opened for a number of national recording acts. In 1967, members of two popular Connecticut groups—the Bram Rigg Set and the Shags—formed a band called Pulse.

Sting

As a solo musician, Sting performed at Oakdale on three occasions. He also played at the Mohegan Sun (seven times) and Foxwoods. He was inducted into the Songwriters Hall of Fame in 2002. Sting and his band the Police performed at the Shaboo Inn, New Haven Coliseum and Hartford Civic Center (three times). The Police were inducted into the Rock 'n' Roll Hall of Fame in 2003.

Kelly Clarkson

Kelly Clarkson performed at the Oakdale on two occasions. She also played at Mohegan Sun (six times), Foxwoods and Meadows Music Theatre (two times).

From the Coliseum to the Shaboo

Sting, Kelly Clarkson and Britney Spears performed at Oakdale. *Courtesy of Live Nation/ Oakdale vice president of marketing, Connecticut and Upstate New York, Jim Bozzi.*

Britney Spears

Britney Spears played at the Oakdale on September 3, 1999. She also performed at Mohegan Sun (three times), Meadows Music Theatre and Hartford Civic Center (twice).

Perry Como

Nicknamed "Mr. C," fan-favorite Perry Como performed at the Oakdale Theatre for six straight days (July 30–August 4, 1979).

TOAD'S PLACE

Back in 1976, our group Eight To The Bar was performing regularly at a restaurant called Hungry Charlie's in New Haven. After one particular gig ended, I knew the back wall was going to be demolished to create a brand new club. I asked the owner Mike Spoerndle if I could be the first one to knock down that wall. Big Mike, who was much amused, said sure. So, still in my fancy dress and in front of a crowd of people, I took

the sledgehammer from Mike. I swung back and hit the wall as hard as I could. Absolutely nothing happened to the wall, not even a dent! My arms and shoulders felt like they had been hit with a sledgehammer, they hurt like hell! Mike laughed and began knocking down the wall himself. That night, local history was made. Tearing down that wall began the conversion of Hungry Charlie's to Mike's new club, which he named "Toad's Place"
—Barbara Lyon, of Eight to the Bar

I've been lucky enough to have played in ALL the fifty states as well as in fifty-two countries around the world, but it's always great to play right here in Connecticut. It's so cool for me to think that I first played Toad's Place in New Haven back in 1980 with Edgar Winter, then twenty odd years later I found myself playing there with Johnny Winter as well…BIG fun!
—Scott Spray

Toad's Place is one of the country's premier music venues, hosting major national recording acts as well as local artists. Recording artists such as Bob Dylan, Bon Jovi, U2, NRBQ, the Ramones, Johnny Winter, Bruce Springsteen, the Reducers, Rick Derringer, Meat Loaf, Eight to the Bar and the Talking Heads have played at Toad's.

The original owner of Toad's Place, Mike Spoerndle, was a native of Cleveland, Ohio. As noted in the *Yale Alumni Magazine*, "Back in Cleveland, 'toad' was used to describe someone who never left the house. Dubbing the restaurant 'Toad's Place' seemed to Spoerndle to sum up his goal of attracting a new crowd."

Other artists who performed at Toad's Place:

The Flying Tigers

One night, during a Flying Tigers show at Toad's, I overenthusiastically grabbed the fire extinguisher off the wall and sprayed the crowd, who loved it! The venue said we would never play there again, even though the next day I took the fire extinguisher to the Fire Department for a fresh refill. And so, the Flying Tigers did lots of shows at a nearby venue called the Oxford Ale House.
—Hall of Famer Dennis Dunaway,
cofounder of Alice Cooper (the group) and the Flying Tigers

The Flying Tigers came on the scene just up the road from me around four years after the Alice Cooper band broke up—which was devastating to me.

Neal initially started the Neal Smith band with David Stackman, Paul Roy and a bass player named Wally. One weekend, Dennis and Cindy Dunaway showed up in a club in Connecticut and Neal met them at the door. I went up, introduced myself and said: "Dennis should be in the band." Next thing I knew, they came back maybe less than a month later with Dennis on bass and a new name: The Flying Tigers. It's true!!!

When I saw the Tigers at Toad's, I really could not believe that my heroes Dennis Dunaway and Neal Smith were five feet in front of me on stage every weekend from 1978 to 1980, and that I was dancing with Cindy Dunaway!

—Weaver Santaniello

After the Alice Cooper band dissolved, band member Neal Smith formed the Flying Tigers. He brought along with him Dennis Dunaway, who was a bandmate of Neal's with the Alice Cooper group. Dennis Dunaway cofounded the Alice Cooper band. Also joining the Flying Tigers were Paul Roy and David Stackman.

In addition to Toad's Place, the Flying Tigers performed at the nearby Oxford Ale House, Norwalk's Night Owl, an outdoor fest called Pinetop and many others. Joe Bouchard and his brother Albert Bouchard (who were former members of Blue Öyster Cult) eventually teamed up with Dennis Dunaway to form the band Blue Coupe.

Flying Tigers, *left to right*: David Stackman, Neal Smith, Paul Roy and Dennis Dunaway. *Courtesy of Fred Fisher.*

HISTORIC CONNECTICUT MUSIC VENUES

The Rolling Stones Impromptu Concert at Toad's Place

Keith Richards and Mick Jagger. *Copyright Ivor Levene.*

On August 12, 1989, the Rolling Stones appeared at Toad's Place for an impromptu concert. The Stones performed eleven songs, beginning with "Start Me Up" and ending with "Jumping Jack Flash," in a concert that lasted nearly an hour. Their appearance at Toad's was a complete surprise to the seven hundred fans who came to listen to local bands, including the group Sons of Bob, which, as it turned out, was the opening act for the Stones that night.

After rehearsing for their "Steel Wheels" tour in the rural town of Washington, Connecticut, the Stones wanted to play in a small music venue to fine-tune some of their new songs, since it had been eight years since their last performance. With the assistance of legendary rock promoter Jimmy Koplik and owner Mike Spoerndle, Toad's Place was selected as the music venue that night for the Stones.

In 1989, the Rolling Stones were inducted into the Rock 'n' Roll Hall of Fame.

Keith Richards

Hall of Fame singer, songwriter and guitarist Keith Richards has lived in Connecticut for well over twenty-five years. Although he still owns a home in the United Kingdom, his house in Connecticut is his primary residence with his wife, Patti Hansen.

During the period that he has been a Connecticut resident, Richards has recorded a number of solo recordings, in addition to his work with the Rolling Stones. "Wicked as It Seems" by Keith Richards was a Top 20 hit on radio stations such as Atlanta's WKLS.

Keith Richards in concert. *Copyright Ivor Levene.*

Richards has also performed in Connecticut, both as a solo artist and as a member of the Rolling Stones. Some of these performances were impromptu stage appearances. For example, Richards joined Willie Nelson on stage for several numbers at the Levitt Pavilion. Also, Richards joined a blues musician for an impromptu jam session at a club in Southington in 2004. In addition, Keith Richards and the Rolling Stones performed an impromptu concert at Toad's Place on August 12, 1989.

Billy Joel

Billy Joel performed at Toad's Place on July 9–10, 1980. In 1999, Ray Charles inducted Billy Joel into the Rock 'n' Roll Hall of Fame.

Lenny Kravitz

International rock star Lenny Kravitz performed at Toad's Place on March 26, 1990. Lenny also performed at the Mohegan Sun (twice) and Foxwoods Theater on two occasions. Among his many awards, Lenny received the Grammy Award for Best Male Rock Vocal Performance four years in a row.

Tina Weymouth and Chris Frantz (Talking Heads)

Tina Weymouth and her husband, Chris Frantz, have been longtime residents of Fairfield. Tina, Chris and David Byrne formed the new wave band Talking Heads in 1975. The Talking Heads consisted of Byrne (lead vocals, guitar), Weymouth (bass) and Frantz (drums). Jerry Harrison (keyboards, guitar) joined the group in 1977. The band was influential in defining the new wave sound and achieved international success in the 1970s and '80s.

The extensive list of accolades for the Talking Heads is impressive. In 2002, the band was inducted into the Rock 'n' Roll Hall of Fame. *Rolling Stone* magazine has included the Talking Heads in its lists of greatest rock bands, greatest albums and songs that shaped rock 'n' roll.

Even before the Talking Heads disbanded, Weymouth and Frantz formed the new wave band Tom Tom Club in Greenwich in 1981. The Tom Tom Club has recorded many singles, as well as (studio and live) albums. "Wordy

Left: Tina Weymouth; *right*: Chris Frantz. *Both courtesy of Billy Green.*

Rappinghood" (1981) by the Tom Tom Club achieved international success (No. 1 U.S. Dance, No. 1 Belgium, No. 2 Netherlands, No. 3 Spain, No. 7 United Kingdom and so on). "Genius of Love" (1981) was a No. 31 *Billboard* hit (and also an international hit). Also, the Tom Tom Club's version of "Under the Boardwalk" (1982) and "The Man with the Four Way Hips" (1983) were international hits.

The Tom Tom Club performed in Connecticut at Toad's Place (twice), the Ridgefield Playhouse, Lake Compounce, New Britain's the Sting, Fairfield's the Warehouse and Stage One.

Chris Frantz has been a programmer at radio station WPKN in Bridgeport for approximately ten years. The name of his radio show is *Chris Frantz the Talking Head*.

Eight to the Bar

Eight to the Bar (ETTB) was founded in 1975 by Cynthia Lyon and John Brown. Cynthia is the band leader, keyboard player and primary songwriter and arranger. She describes her group as "a band that plays swing with a rock sensibility."

The original ETTB lineup consisted of Cynthia Lyon with her sisters Todd Lyon and Barbara Lyon, Rob Jockel, Tom McNamara, John Brown, John Baker and Matt Simpson. The current lineup is Cynthia Lyon, Collin Tilton, Brinna Jones, Kevin Johnson, Eric Kuhn and Justin Blackburn

ETTB has performed at Hungry Charlie's/Toad's Place over fifty times! The group has also played in other Connecticut music venues, including the Shaboo Inn. In addition, ETTB has performed throughout the United States and all over the world, including the Republic of Georgia and many countries in Europe.

Moby

Moby has played at Connecticut music venues such as Toad's Place and Meadows Music Theatre.

Michael Bolton (aka Michael Bolotin)

Singer-songwriter Michael Bolton was born Michael Bolotin in New Haven. Bolton's father, George, and mother, Helen, were also born in New Haven. As a boy, he lived with his family in several New Haven locations, including homes on Whalley Avenue, Elm Street and Ella Grasso Boulevard.

Prior to becoming the singing sensation known to millions of his loyal fans, Bolton was active in the New Haven music scene. At an early age, Bolton began composing songs. As a teenager, he performed and recorded as a solo artist under his given name Bolotin. He then became a member of a garage rock group called Joy, under the name Bolotin. "Bah Bah Bah" by Joy was a Top 40 hit in Connecticut. Bolotin (Bolton) was also the lead singer of the heavy metal band known as Blackjack. "Love Me Tonight" by Blackjack was a Top 20 hit on Buffalo's WYSL radio station and in several other markets. Recordings took place at Wallingford's Trod Nossel studios. The band opened for major artists, such as Peter Frampton. Blackjack performed in various music venues in the New Haven area such as Toad's Place.

Bolton went on to become the rock/soul icon Michael Bolton. Bolton has sold over seventy-five million records and won numerous impressive awards, including Grammys.

There is somewhat of a connection between Michael Bolton and the popular 1960s band the Shags. Michael's older brother Orrin was a roadie for the Shags, and Orrin introduced Michael to the band. Allegedly, Carl Augusto/Donnell (a member of the Shags) helped teach young Michael how to play the guitar.

Debbie Davies

Singer, songwriter and guitarist Debbie Davies is a blues extraordinaire who moved to Connecticut's Fairfield County in 1994 because of the welcoming blues scene in the state. As noted by Thomas Staudter in a *New York Times* article, "Connecticut at Its Best: Where the Music That 'Opens Your Soul' Has a Home," on December 12, 2004, "Ms. Davies, who lives near Bridgeport, is a past winner of the W.C. Handy Award for top contemporary female blues artist of the year. Between sets she remarked that blues bookings on the East Coast have always been plentiful, and that she had moved to Connecticut from her native California 10 years ago 'because the blues scene here had a lot of energy and a good reputation.'" Some of the Connecticut clubs that have featured blues artists like Davies are Black-Eyed Sally's, Hungry Tiger and Toad's Place.

According to her website, Debbie has released fifteen albums and two collaborative CDs. Her latest release is the 2015 blues CD *Love Spin*. Among her many honors were the 1997 and 2010 Best Contemporary Female Blues Artist awards. Debbie Davies has shared the stage and recording studio with some of the greatest and most respected blues artists in the United States.

Hardknox

The Hardknox band opened for Michael Bolotin (aka Michael Bolton) at Toad's Place on September 7, 1978. Hardknox featured the talented Wayne Gamache, Tom Marak and Tony Rondini.

Hardknox band. *Photo by John Stillwell; courtesy of Wayne Gamache of Hardknox.*

Napi Browne

Napi Browne was a hard rock band formed in New Haven in 1976. The band included North Haven's singer-songwriter Paul Rosano, who was previously a member of two popular Connecticut bands: Bram Rigg Set and Pulse. Band members included Rosano (bass, vocals), Vic Steffens, (drums, background vocals), Nick Bagnasco (guitar, vocals) and Dan Gulino (guitar, background vocals). Steffens is the brother of rocker Christine Ohlman

Napi Browne performed at numerous music venues in Connecticut, including Toad's Place. The band's touring area included New England and New York. Napi Browne recorded songs at Paul Leka's Studios in Bridgeport. Songwriters for the band included Rosano, Bagnasco and Gulino. Their song "Let's Get Right to It" was a track on WHCN's *Homespun* album (1980).

Napi Browne was a popular band in the late 1970s and early 1980s.

Thurston Moore

Singer, songwriter and guitarist Thurston Moore moved with his family to Bethel when Thurston was nine years old. He and his family lived on Codfish Hill in Bethel. He spent his childhood and high school years in Connecticut. Moore attended St. Joseph Elementary School in Danbury. He then transferred to and graduated from Bethel's St. Mary Elementary School. At an early age, Thurston was involved in social activities in and around the Bethel area. According to the May 12, 1970 edition of the *Bridgeport Post*, fifth grader Thurston Moore volunteered to clean up a park at the intersection of Codfish Hill and Wolfpits Road as part of Bethel's "Operation Clean Up" initiative. He was also a Cub Scout at the time. According to the July 1, 1971 edition of the *Bridgeport Post*, Thurston participated in a St. Mary School project in which he helped produce a film on the drug problems in and around Bethel. Thurston then attended Bethel High School, graduating class of 1976. It was in high school that Thurston developed his musical tastes and passion for rock 'n' roll. His high school yearbook writeup referred to him as a "rock 'n' roll animal." Thurston applied and was accepted to Danbury's Western Connecticut State University (WCSU) in 1976. After spending a semester at WCSU, Moore moved to New York City, where he became actively involved in the progressive rock music scene there.

In 1981, Moore formed the alternative rock band Sonic Youth along with Kim Gordon and Lee Ranaldo. Thurston and Kim married in 1984. Sonic

Youth consisted mainly of Moore (singer, songwriter, guitarist), Gordon (vocals, bass guitar) and Ranaldo (guitar, vocals). Over the years, other musicians joined Sonic Youth.

Sonic Youth disbanded in 2011. During the period between 1981 and 2011, Sonic Youth released an extensive number of singles, albums, EPs and compilation albums. Thurston Moore has been recognized several times in *Rolling Stone* magazine as one of the top guitarists in the United States.

Sonic Youth performed at a number of music venues in Connecticut, including Oakdale, Toad's Place, Meadows Music Theatre, New Haven's Palace Theatre and the Hartford Civic Center.

The Simms Brothers

In 1979, the very popular New Haven radio station WPLR conducted a poll of its listeners to determine the best band in Connecticut. The Simms Brothers Band was voted Connecticut's number one act. The group's self-titled album did well on the East Coast (No. 18 on Boston's radio station WBCN). The band performed at various Connecticut music venues, such as the Players Tavern and Toad's Place. The Simms Brothers formed in 1974 in Stamford.

Over the years, members of the Simms Brothers included Frank Simms, George Simms, Steve Simms, Budd Tunick, Dave Spinner, Dennis Collins, John Van Epps, Mickey Leonard, Pat Rustici, Rob Sabino, Shimmy Maki and Ted MacKenzie,

Prior to the formation of the Simms Brothers band, Mickey Leonard was a member of the Wheels. In 1964, the Wheels were the opening act for the D-Men at Stamford's Ezio Pinza music venue, a three-thousand-seat outdoor amphitheater. Bob Klein was also a member of the Wheels before joining the Fifth Estate band. Also on the bill at Ezio Pinza was the group the Malibus. Frank Simms and Budd Tunick played with the Malibus and eventually became members of the Simms Brothers band.

Blake Street Gut Band

The Blake Street Gut Band was a popular local Connecticut act from 1969 to 1975. During this six-year period, the band members consisted of David "Bobo" Lavorgna (bass/vocals), Matthew Elgosin, John Menta, Armand Morgan, Michael Ferrucci, Steve Ditzell, Peter Menta, Ken Rieske and

Bernie Soroko. The Blake Street Gut Band performed in a number of local music venues in Connecticut, including Hungry Charlie's (which became Toad's Place).

Mohegan Sun

The Mohegan Sun has been a very big part of my life after the Rascals disbanded.
—Felix Cavaliere

A world at play and a world to its own.
—Mohegan Sun slogan

Love the Mohegan Sun! I was in the first band to ever play the Wolf Den at Mohegan Sun (Jay Stollman & the All Stars). We played five nights a week for six weeks at a time. This was before the hotel was built, so there was a lot of driving back and forth—but it was worth it!

Later on, of course, I played there with Johnny Winter and then with Gene Cornish of the Rascals...such a great music venue to play in.
—Scott Spray

The Mohegan Sun in Uncasville, Connecticut, opened in 1996 and has hosted numerous major recording artists, including Eric Clapton (five times), the Rascals, Chuck Berry, Little Richard (twice), Meat Loaf (six times), John Mayer, Peter & Gordon and the Alcatrazz band.

Other notable performances at the Mohegan Sun:

Brian Wilson

As noted on Brian Wilson's website, legendary Hall of Fame singer/songwriter/record producer Brian Wilson is considered "one of the most influential composers of the last century." Brian Wilson (along with his group the Beach Boys) was inducted by Elton John into the Rock 'n' Roll Hall of Fame in 1988 and the Songwriters Hall of Fame in 2001.

Brian Wilson performed on his birthday at Mohegan Sun on June 20, 1999. To celebrate his birthday, Brian was presented a large cake, and the entire audience sang "Happy Birthday," to his delight. Brian also performed at the Mohegan Sun on July 11, 2000 (Pet Sounds Tour), and January 23, 2020.

Brian Wilson at Mohegan Sun on June 20, 1999. *Author's collection.*

Ronnie Spector

Ronnie Spector and I go back a long way. She is a dear friend of mine and what an amazing talent! She's such a special person who I am very fond of.

—*Felix Cavaliere*

Legendary Ronnie Spector has lived in Danbury area for over twenty years. During this period, Spector has released seven solo albums, including *English Heart*, released on April 8, 2016.

Ronnie has performed in concert in Connecticut many times, including the Mohegan Sun (eleven times), the Ridgefield Playhouse (twice), the New Haven Green (July 21, 2018), Danbury Ives Concert Park (2011) and Norfolk's Infinity Hall.

Ronnie Spector achieved fame as a member of the Ronettes, recording such great hits as "Be My Baby" and "Baby, I Love You." According to Ronnie's website, "Be My Baby" was named by *Billboard* as the "No.1 Greatest Girl Group Song of All-Time." The Ronettes were discovered by DJ Murray the K and produced by Phil Spector (Ronnie's ex-husband). Ronnie and the Ronettes were inducted into the Rock 'n' Roll Hall of Fame in 2007.

Ronnie Spector's personal note to author and the Ronettes photos. *Courtesy of Ronnie Spector and author's collection.*

Gene Pitney

Legendary singer/songwriter Gene Pitney performed at the Mohegan Sun on March 30, 2003. He played in many other music venues in Connecticut. Pitney was inducted by Darlene Love into the Rock 'n' Roll Hall of Fame in 2002. Darlene Love was the lead singer of the Crystals' No. 1 song, "He's a Rebel," written by Pitney. Gene Pitney was born in Hartford and raised in Rockville, Connecticut where he earned the name the "Rockville Rocket."

Gene Pitney recording at his home studio. *Courtesy of the Gene Pitney Commemorative Committee.*

Ringo Starr

Ringo Starr. *Copyright Ivor Levene.*

Ringo Starr is a perfect example of guys from the '60s who just love to play music. I mean, you got to get the hook to get him off the stage, he loves music that much! He is an iconic artist but more importantly a wonderful human being. It was really great working with him as part of his All-Starr tour, playing at the Oakdale and many other music venues across the country. He's the real thing and such a nice guy!

—Felix Cavaliere

Ringo Starr performed at the Mohegan Sun (with his All-Starr Band) on more than ten occasions.

Alanis Morissette

Alanis Morissette. *Copyright Philamonjaro.*

Alanis Morissette performed at the Mohegan Sun on three occasions. Alanis also played at Foxwoods Theatre (two times), Waterbury's Palace Theatre, Oakdale, the Xfinity Theatre and Meadows Music Theatre.

The Yardbirds

The Yardbirds have performed at Mohegan Sun on six occasions. The band played at various other music venues, including the Infinity Hall (two times) and Westport's Staples High School (October 22, 1966). Note: The concert at Staples High School is notable because it featured the Yardbirds with both Jimmy Page and Jeff Beck. Page and Beck played together with the Yardbirds only that one year (1966). Also, the Yardbirds concert at Staples was the first date of their 1966 tour.

Jeff Beck (who performed with the Yardbirds in 1966) along with Steven Tyler (Aerosmith). *Copyright Ivor Levene.*

Johnny Winter

Easton's Johnny Winter with Scott Spray on bass, Mohegan Sun Wolf Den, January 7, 2011. *Courtesy of Andrea Spray.*

From the Coliseum to the Shaboo

INFINITY HALL HARTFORD/NORFOLK

I have been fortunate in recent years to see many bands in a variety of Connecticut music venues. My favorite band is the Zombies. I saw them perform a number of songs from the album Odessey and Oracle *at Hartford's Infinity Hall on July 15, 2017. Rod Argent shared how the Zombies recorded the album at Abbey Road Studios shortly after The Beatles recorded* Sgt. Pepper's Lonely Hearts Club Band. *They even used some of the instruments that the Beatles had used in their own recordings that were still in the studio. I also saw the Zombies when they shared the stage with another of my musical heroes, Brian Wilson, at Waterbury's Palace Theater in Waterbury on September 27, 2019. As an eligible voter of the Rock 'n' Roll Hall of Fame, I was delighted to cast my vote for the Zombies when they were inducted in 2019.*

—*David Miller*

Infinity Music Hall Hartford has a seating capacity of five hundred and is located on 32 Front Street. Infinity Music Hall Norfolk has a seating capacity of three hundred and is located on 20 Greenwoods Road West. Both music venues host a variety of well-known national artists and bands, such as Felix Cavaliere's Rascals, Ronnie Spector, Blue Coupe and Johnny Winter.

Other notable performances at Infinity Hall (Hartford and Norfolk):

The Zombies

The Zombies performed at Hartford's Infinity Hall on July 15, 2017. In 2019, the Zombies were inducted into the Rock 'n' Roll Hall of Fame.

The Zombies in concert.
Copyright Philamonjaro.

Historic Connecticut Music Venues

Denny Laine

Denny Laine performed at the Infinity Hall (Norfolk and Hartford). Laine was formerly a member of the Moody Blues and Paul McCartney's band. The Moody Blues (including Denny Laine) were inducted into the Rock 'n' Roll Hall of Fame on August 13, 2018.

Meadows Music Theatre

Xfinity Theatre (The Meadows) was built by me and Shelly Finkel in 1995. I consider it the preeminent outdoor concert venue in Connecticut's history as most great artists have played there including the Eagles, Elton John, Bob Dylan, Paul Simon, Bruce Springsteen and so many more. It also hosted the 2018 and 2021 Farm Aid concerts. But the most amazing fact is that the Dave Matthews Band played there forty-one times
—*Jim Koplik, Live Nation president*

Hartford's Meadows Music Theatre has undergone several name changes and is now known as the Xfinity Theatre. Prior venue names were the New England Dodge Music Center and Comcast Theatre. Many people still refer to this music venue as The Meadows.

This music venue holds a total of 30,000 fans (22,500 outdoors and 7,500 indoors). Meadows/Xfinity Theatre has played host to numerous major recording artists, such as Bob Dylan and Paul Simon (coheadliners), Brian Wilson with Paul Simon, Felix Cavaliere and Tom Petty.

Other notable performances at Meadows Music Theatre:

Snoop Dogg

Snoop Dogg performed at The Meadows Music Theatre on four occasions. Snoop also played at the Oakdale Theatre on January 17, 2020.

Dave Matthews

Dave Matthews has performed at The Meadows on forty-one occasions. He has also played at other Connecticut music venues, including the New Haven Coliseum, Mohegan Sun, Hartford Civic and Oakdale Theatre.

Jack Johnson

Jack Johnson performed at The Meadows/Comcast Theatre on July 9, 2010.

Taylor Swift

Taylor Swift played at The Meadows/New England Dodge Music Center on August 22, 2008. Taylor also performed at Mohegan Sun (five times) and the XL Center.

John Mayer

Singer, songwriter and guitarist John Mayer was born in Bridgeport and raised in Fairfield, Connecticut. His father, Richard, was the principal of Bridgeport's Central High School. His mother, Margaret, was a middle school English teacher in the Bridgeport area.

Mayer attended a magnet program at Norwalk's Brien McMahon High School called the Center for Japanese Studies Abroad. Mayer graduated from Fairfield High School (now Fairfield Warde High). At seventeen, Mayer became a member of a Connecticut band called Another Roadside Attraction. The band played clubs in the local area and recorded some demos.

Top: Dave Matthews. *Copyright Philamonjaro.*

Middle: Jack Johnson. *Copyright Philamonjaro.*

Bottom: Taylor Swift. *Copyright Ivor Levene.*

Historic Connecticut Music Venues

John Mayer. *Copyright Philamonjaro.*

In 1995, Mayer and his Connecticut band known as Villanova Junction (a high school band) recorded a number of songs at Pulse Wave Recording Studios in Trumbull.

Of course, John Mayer has gone on to achieve fame as a major recording artist. His current band experience is with Dead & Company. In a *Rolling Stone* article by David Fricke on June 21, 2016, "John Mayer on Playing with Dead & Company: 'It's Like Catching Air'," Mayer shared his thoughts on performing with members of the Grateful Dead as part of the Dead & Company concerts during the summer of 2016.

Mayer reflected on what an honor it was to be associated with these great musicians and his excitement at the prospect of one day recording with members of the Dead. When asked about his earliest impressions of the Dead as a high school student at Fairfield High School, Mayer responded, "I knew the Grateful Dead as a cultural assignment. I didn't know it as a musical thing. Where I lived, in Fairfield, if you liked the Dead it was like you were issued clothing. I was going to school with the Deadheads' younger brothers. I never looked down on it. I was just into Eric Clapton, Jimi Hendrix and Stevie Ray Vaughan." Mayer has since become immersed in the music of the Grateful Dead and considers his association with the band members to be a major highlight of his career. When asked for his thoughts on John Mayer's participation in Dead & Company, Bob Weir responded, "He gets what we're up to. It appeals to his sense of fun and adventure. Then he brings his musical personality."

John Mayer has played at The Meadows Music Theatre on eight occasions. Mayer performed in his hometown of Bridgeport several times, including the Acoustic Café (June 25, 2001), Harbor Yard (March 17, 2004) and the Webster Bank Arena (December 16, 2013). He also played at Willimantic's Geissler Gymnasium, the Oakdale and Mohegan Sun.

An article in the March 20, 2015 edition of the *Connecticut Post* ("Born and Raised: 10 Things You May Not Know about John Mayer" by Scott Gargan) cites further connections that John Mayer has with his hometown state of Connecticut:

- Mayer's first time on stage was at the Westport Central School talent show.

- He was inspired by his father, Richard, who used to play piano at their home.
- When Mayer was fifteen, he took guitar lessons from Al Ferrante, owner of the Fairfield Guitar Shop.
- Fairfield's Grand Central supermarket was his first ever employer.
- After graduating from Fairfield High School, Mayer spent fifteen months working as an attendant at the Mobil gas station (corner of Fairfield Woods Road and Stratfield Road—across the street from Fairfield's Grand Central Supermarket).
- Mayer donated a guitar to benefit the families of Newtown's Sandy Hook Elementary School.
- In interviews, Mayer has referred to himself as just another "dude from Fairfield."
- He has returned several times to his high school alma mater Fairfield High School (now Fairfield Warde High School), one of which was to attend the ten-year reunion of his graduating class.

FOXWOODS THEATRE

As a high school student, I had the wonderful opportunity to see the Beatles perform live in concert at Shea Stadium. I will never forget the thrill, excitement, and true hysteria that was felt throughout the venue as the Beatles took the stage. If not for that music venue and for the countless music venues that have arisen in Connecticut and across the country, music fans would be deprived of the sheer joy of seeing their favorite band performing live in concert.
—Julia Fleischmann

The wonder of it all.
—Foxwoods slogan

The Foxwoods Theatre in Mashantucket, Connecticut, has played host to numerous major recording artists, including Frank Sinatra, Gene Pitney, Brian Wilson, Little Richard, Mavis Staples and Chuck Berry.

Other notable performances at Foxwoods:

Ringo Starr

Ringo Starr & His All-Starr Band performed at Foxwoods on July 27, 1995, and October 24, 2015. Ringo also performed in a number of other Connecticut music venues, including the Oakdale Theatre (three times), Mohegan Sun (over ten times) and Lake Compounce (August 2, 1989).

Ringo Starr was inducted into the rock 'n' roll Hall of Fame as a member of the Beatles in 1988.

Ringo Starr. *Copyright Philamonjaro.*

Diana Ross

Diana Ross has resided in Greenwich, Connecticut, for over fifteen years. She has appeared as a solo performer in a number of Connecticut music venues, including Foxwoods (seventeen times), Oakdale (six times), Bushnell Memorial (two times), Stamford's Palace Theater (two times), Hartford Civic Center (two times) and Lake Compounce.

As a solo artist, Diana has had six No. 1 songs on the *Billboard* charts. Ross was named the "Female Entertainer of the Century' by Billboard in 1976. She is the only female artist to have No. 1 singles on the *Billboard* Hot 100 as a solo artist, as the other half of a duet, as a member of a trio and as an ensemble member. *Billboard* ranked her as the 28th greatest Hot 100 artist of all time.

Diana Ross and the Supremes were inducted into the Rock 'n' Roll Hall of Fame in 1988. Diana was the recipient of the Grammys' Lifetime Achievement Award in 2012 (her first Grammy award).

Sheryl Crow

Sheryl Crow performed at Foxwoods on three occasions. Sheryl also played at Meadows Music Theatre (six times), Foxwoods (three times), Mohegan Sun (two times), the Bushnell and Oakdale.

Sheryl Crow. *Copyright Ivor Levene.*

Johnny Winter

Blues legend Johnny Winter was a guitarist, singer, songwriter and producer who moved to Easton, Connecticut, in 1999. He lived in Easton for fifteen years prior to his death in 2014. During the period that Winter lived in Connecticut, he released nine albums (studio and live) and seven compilation albums. In 2003, Winter was recognized by *Rolling Stone* magazine as one of the greatest guitarists in the United States. In 2004, his *I'm a Bluesman* album received a Grammy nomination. And in 2015, *Step Back*, released posthumously, won the Grammy for "Best Blues Album."

Winter has performed in many Connecticut music venues such as the Agora Ballroom, the Shaboo Inn, the Waterbury Palace Theatre, Toad's Place, Webster Theatre, Infinity Hall, Mohegan Sun, the Fairfield Theatre, the Ridgefield Playhouse and Foxwoods.

Winter is probably best known for his electrifying live performances and his high-energy blues/rock albums. Johnny Winter performed for over an hour on the third day of the original Woodstock Festival in August 1969. At Woodstock, he performed such songs as his amazing "Mean Town Blues" and "Tobacco Road" (with his brother Edgar Winter as lead singer).

During his incredible career, Winter recorded nearly thirty studio and live albums and earned many Grammy nominations (plus a posthumous Grammy Award in 2015).

Johnny Winter is buried in Easton, Connecticut, at Union Cemetery.

Toto

The rock band Toto included brothers Jeff, Mike and Steve Porcaro, all talented musicians. All three Porcaro brothers were born in the South Windsor–Hartford, Connecticut area: Steve (keyboards, composer, vocals), Jeff (drums, percussions) and Mike (bass, backing vocals).

The Porcaro brothers were part of a very musical family. Their father, Joe Porcaro, and mother, Eileen Linnell Porcaro, were musicians in the Hartford Symphony. Joe played percussion, and Eileen played flute. Moreover, Joe Porcaro became a well-known and well-respected professional jazz drummer and percussionist. The family eventually moved to California, where the Porcaro brothers and their group Toto achieved national fame. Toto performed at Foxwoods in August 2015.

THE HARTFORD HEALTHCARE AMPHITHEATER (BRIDGEPORT, CONNECTICUT)

The Hartford HealthCare Amphitheater is one of the premier boutique amphitheaters in the country.

—*Jim Koplik, Live Nation president, Connecticut and Upstate New York*

I had a wonderful experience attending my first concert at the brand-new Hartford Healthcare Amphitheater in Bridgeport. The concert featured both the Beach Boys and Felix Cavaliere's Rascals. This music venue offers very comfortable seating, great views, and a terrific sound system. In addition, the Amphitheater is conveniently located off the main highways I-95 and Route 8. It was such a wonderful experience to once again attend a live concert in a music venue. I loved the audience vibe and also the fan reaction that only a live concert can offer.

—*Russ Pettinicchi*

From the Coliseum to the Shaboo

Hartford Healthcare Amphitheater. *Courtesy of Jim Koplik, Live Nation president.*

The brand-new, luxurious 5,700-plus seat Hartford Healthcare Amphitheater is located in Bridgeport, Connecticut, and opened in the summer of 2021. According to the website https://hartfordhealthcareamp.com, the amphitheater is a joint venture between the City of Bridgeport and Hartford HealthCare Amphitheater in association with Live Nation.

The Bridgeport amphitheater hosted notable artists in 2021, including Alice Cooper, the Beach Boys, Felix Cavaliere, Little Big Town and many others.

CHARLES ROSENAY CONVENTIONS

As far as I'm concerned, my life began on February 9, 1964, when the Beatles first appeared on The Ed Sullivan Show. *It's actually my first memory in life and nothing was the same after that. Obviously, I couldn't be a Beatle, but it is a godsend that I found a way to entertain people and channel my love of music and the Beatles into a lifestyle and a profession.*
—*Charles Rosenay, producer*

Charles F. Rosenay of New Haven is a producer, actor, entertainer, MC/DJ, tour organizer and music/horror aficionado. While still in his teens, Charles founded Liverpool Productions to promote Beatles conventions and to start his DJ entertainment company. This branched out to include organizing Magical History Tours of the Beatles' attractions in Liverpool and London, England.

Rosenay also published his own Beatles magazine called *Good Day Sunshine*, which became one of the most-read Beatles publications in the world. He also produces conventions for Monkees fans. Charles F. Rosenay has presented conventions throughout Connecticut (and many other locations) from 1978 through the present time, hosting an array of major recording artists and celebrities.

The following are some of the artists that have appeared at the Charles Rosenay Conventions in Connecticut and Liverpool Tours:

Above, left: Richie Havens, Beatles Convention, 1983; *right*: Micky Dolenz (of the Monkees). *Both courtesy of Charles Rosenay, producer.*

Left: Linda McCartney, Rosenay's Liverpool Tours. *Courtesy of Charles Rosenay, producer.*

3
CONNECTICUT BANDSTAND
TV DANCE SHOW

I was fortunate to be a member of the singing group called the Academics. We appeared in many Connecticut music venues and the fan reaction was terrific. In 1958, we performed our fan-favorite song "Somethin' Cool" on the popular Connecticut Bandstand *TV show. As we approached the bandstand stage, the girls were screaming so loud that it was difficult to hear the intro for our song. The sound was deafening! But it was a lot of fun, and I have such good memories of that show and the other Connecticut music venues we performed in.*
—*Marty Ganter, of the Academics*

The Premiers closed out 1960 with a guest appearance on the Connecticut Bandstand *New Year's Special show on WNHC-TV. Bobby "Boris" Pickett was also on the show's lineup. Of course, he did his famous "Monster Mash," which was sort of weird for a New Year's Eve show, but it worked out well. The Premiers did our popular songs "Pigtails Eyes Are Blue" and "I Pray." A fun experience! I think that was the only New Year's Eve show that* Connecticut Bandstand *ever produced.* Connecticut Bandstand *was a very popular TV dance show for teenagers, and Jim Gallant treated guests on his show in a very professional manner.*
—*Bill Koob, of the Premiers*

I went to Connecticut Bandstand *with a bunch of my friends from Sacred Heart High School in Waterbury. We had a blast, and it was so much fun dancing and watching the performers singing on the show. Every once in a while*

Historic Connecticut Music Venues

we would take a quick peek at the monitor and see ourselves and the other kids while we were dancing. Our families and friends tuned in to watch us on the TV show—and, of course, everything was shown in black and white!
—Paula Renzoni Crean

On July 9, 1956, Dick Clark took over as host of *American Bandstand* on WFIL-TV in Philadelphia, Pennsylvania. Later that same year (October 17, 1956), WNHC-TV in New Haven began airing *Connecticut Bandstand*. Both WFIL and WNHC were station affiliates under the Triangle Publications Radio and Television company.

For the most part, *Connecticut Bandstand* mirrored Dick Clark's national *American Bandstand*. The show's format featured teenagers in and around Connecticut who danced to hit songs that were popular at the time. Local pop artists from Connecticut performed on the show, lip-syncing to their recordings. Like *American Bandstand*, the *Connecticut Bandstand* show featured dance regulars who gained local fame and even had their own fan clubs. Two such regulars were a couple known as Cookie and Charley. Cookie Teznick and Charley (Charlie) Lent were a popular dancing duo on the show in 1957. Later that year, Cookie and Charley recorded two singles—"Let's Go Rock and Roll" and "I Love You So"—that were popular on a local basis, charting in the Top 20 on Connecticut radio stations. The duo performed at the New Haven Arena on May 8, 1958, as part of Alan Freed's Big Beat Show at the Arena. Many of the teenagers appearing on the show were students at local New Haven high schools, such as Hillhouse High and Wilbur Cross High.

Local recording artists who performed on *Connecticut Bandstand* included Debbie and the Darnels, the Catalinas, the Academics, Ginny Arnell, Andy Dio, Billy James, Roger Koob and the Premiers, the Van Dykes, the Reveliers, the Pyramids and Ron and His Rattletones. Also, famed actor Vincent Price was a guest on the October 22, 1956 episode of *Connecticut Bandstand*.

Connecticut Bandstand aired on WNHC-TV weekdays Monday through Friday at 3:30 p.m., immediately prior to *American Bandstand*. The show's first host was Jim Gallant. He was born on Christmas Eve 1930 in Marion, Ohio. Gallant hosted many record hops and outdoor shows featuring local performers. For example, Gallant hosted and produced concerts at Bristol's Lake Compounce and at Marino's Danz-Er-Roll in Buckingham Hall in Waterbury (1959). Also, it is purported that Gallant was in the running to host *American Bandstand*, but the job was awarded to Dick Clark. After allegations of payola arose, Gallant resigned in protest, refusing to sign an affidavit admitting to receiving gifts in exchange for playing records. In

March 1960, Elliot "Biggie" Nevins became the show's new host. Nevins also hosted local record hops. *Connecticut Bandstand* ended in 1962, with Mike Sapack as the last host of the show. *Connecticut Bandstand* was a popular TV show for viewers around the state.

Direct Connection between *Connecticut Bandstand* and *American Bandstand*

Here is a document that shows a direct connection between *Connecticut Bandstand and American Bandstand*. The letter is typewritten (of course) and dated February 17, 1961.

This is a letter of recommendation to *American Bandstand* (Philadelphia, Pennsylvania) from and signed by Elliot "Biggie" Nevins, on behalf of one of the regulars of *Connecticut Bandstand* (WNHC-TV, New Haven). Biggie Nevins was the host of *Connecticut Bandstand* at the time. Biggie replaced host Jim Gallant.

The letter from Nevins requests consideration for a longtime *Connecticut Bandstand* regular (Joseph "Foo" De Martino) to be part of the *American Bandstand* show during the week mentioned.

Note: As shown, this letter to *American Bandstand* has the annotation "Okay for week of April 24, 1961. W.H. Mallery." Of note, W.H. "Bill" Mallery was Barbara Mallery's brother (as confirmed by AB historian Charles Amann). Barbara Mallery was Dick Clark's first wife.

The typewritten envelope (not shown) is addressed to *American Bandstand*, WFIL-TV. On the back of the envelope (not shown) that contained the letter are names and addresses of *American Bandstand* "contacts" for De Martino once he got to Philadelphia. He was to meet *American Bandstand* regulars Susan Beltrante and Carolyn DeSimine.

This document is significant for the following reasons:

1. The documents show the link between *Connecticut Bandstand* (a local bandstand TV show) and the national *American Bandstand* TV show
2. The importance and significance given to being a regular on *American Bandstand* since Susan Beltrante, Carolyn DeSimine were chosen as the *American Bandstand* "ambassadors" as they were to be De Martino's contact upon his arrival in Philadelphia

Letter from Biggie Nevins of *Connecticut Bandstand* to *American Bandstand*, February 17, 1961. *Author's collection.*

3. W.H. (Bill) Mallery's involvement with the *American Bandstand* show
4. Confirmation that both WFIL and WNHC were station affiliates under the Triangle Publications Radio and Television company (as noted at the bottom of the letter).

I asked a noted *American Bandstand* expert (the late Charles Amann) for his thoughts and clarification of this letter. Amann had a popular blog about *American Bandstand* and knew many of the shows "regulars." I emailed a copy of the letter Amann for his thoughts and any clarification needed. His response was as follows:

Tony,

Bill Mallery was Dick Clark's wife Barbara's brother and employed by the show. Truly, this is marvelous as a Historical Reference! I will be doing a blog on this and adding this to the archives. I am grateful that you have shared this with me. I know the fans are going to love it! I am close with all the Regulars, personal friends with many. I will most certainly send your regards. I have attached a copy of a photo of Susie Beltrante (One of the three Beltrante sisters, Rosalie and Mary, the others) and Caroline DeSimine. My book on American Bandstand is yet to be released. I will put you on the mailing list when it is ready for the shelves and see you get a personal copy. Very Best Regards,
Charles

Sadly, Charles Amann passed away prior to the completion of his book.

The following are some of the artists who performed on *Connecticut Bandstand*:

The Academics

The Academics were a vocal harmony group that formed while the group members were attending Hillhouse High School in New Haven. The group originally called the Tri-Tones was made up of Marty Ganter, Billy Greenberg, and Ronnie Marrone. Their name was changed to the Academics when they expanded to five group members. The new name was

HISTORIC CONNECTICUT MUSIC VENUES

The Academics on *Connecticut Bandstand*. *Left to right*: Ron Marone, Billy Greenberg, Marty Ganter, Charlie Luth and Dave Fisher. *Courtesy of Marty Ganter (of the Academics)*.

chosen as a tribute to Hillhouse High School, since the school's nickname was the Academics.

The Academics' appearance on Jim Gallant's *Connecticut Bandstand* TV show helped their 1957 tune "Too Good to Be True" become a No. 1 song in the New Haven area. "Too Good to Be True" was written and performed by the Academics' Marty Ganter. Another local fan favorite was "Drive-In Movie," written by Ganter and Billy Greenberg and performed by Marty Ganter. The flip side was a Dave Fisher composition called "Somethin' Cool" (performed by Dave Fisher). The Academics performed on *Connecticut Bandstand* on several occasions.

After graduating from Hillhouse High, the Academics' Dave Fisher cofounded the Highwaymen folk group when he was a freshman at Middletown's Wesleyan University. Fisher and the Highwaymen recorded the mega-hit song "Michael Row the Boat Ashore."

From the Coliseum to the Shaboo

Debbie and the Darnels

We performed on the Connecticut Bandstand *TV show around 1963. We sang our songs on the show and got a nice fan reaction. After performing, we signed autographs for the other teenagers who danced on the show, which we were thrilled to do. After all, they were teenagers, about the same age as us!*
—Dorothy Yutenkas, lead singer of Debbie and the Darnels

Dorothy Yutenkas, her sister Joan and a friend, Maria Brancati, made up the singing trio Debbie and the Darnels, which hailed from New Haven. In 1962, the group was known as the Teen Dreams. Later that year, the trio's name was changed to Debbie and the Darnels.

Their upbeat tune "Mr. Johnny Jones" was a Top 40 hit on local Connecticut radio stations. The trio's Christmastime offering was a lively and catchy tune called "Santa Teach Me to Dance."

Dorothy Yutenkas was the lead singer and wrote the group's first recording, "Why." The trio was discovered by New Haven's Jerry Greenberg, who also wrote "The Time" for the group. Backing up the trio was Greenberg's

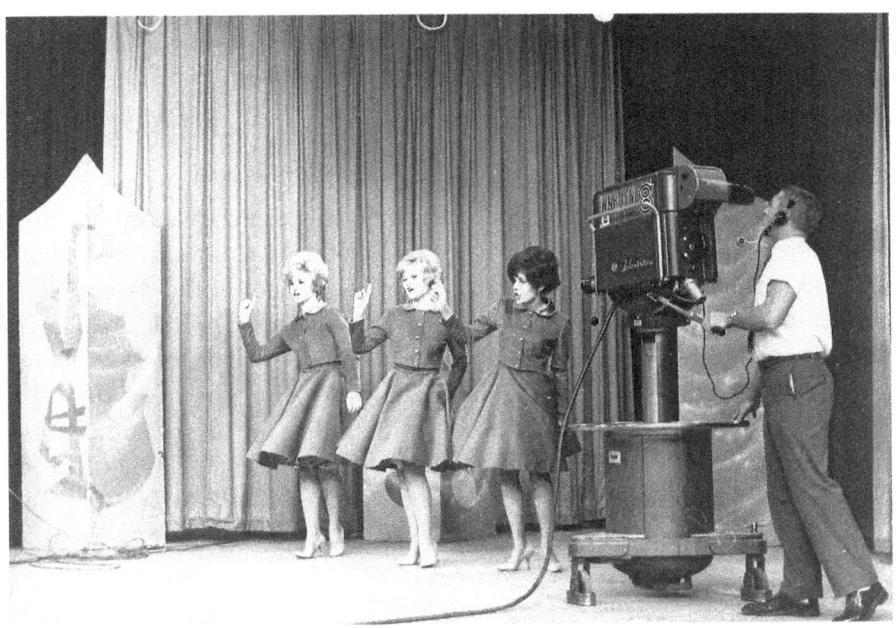

Debbie and the Darnels on *Connecticut Bandstand. Courtesy of Dorothy Yutenkas.*

instrumental band the Passengers. The group was managed by Sam Goldman (manager of the Five Satins).

Dorothy Yutenkas recalled hearing their song on the radio for the first time:

> *I first heard our song on the radio while I was riding in a car on a date. My sister Joan was in the backseat. Our song comes on the car radio, and we just went crazy—screaming and singing along with the song. I thought to myself, "Now we made it." I so remember that moment. It doesn't get any better than that!*

Dorothy also recalled what it was like when the teenage trio appeared on stage at large concert shows:

> *I remember we did a huge show on a very large stage and the announcer introduced us, "Here are Debbie and the Darnels." And all the kids would start screaming, much like they did for groups like the Beatles. It sometimes got a bit scary for us, especially when the teenage boys would start grabbing at our legs and things like that. Girl groups such as ours sometimes would get a little frightened because it sometimes seemed to get a bit chaotic with all the screaming and such. Guys could get a bit aggressive, and we were a bit concerned about that at those large venues. There would be a few bodyguards for us, but not really professional, you know. We were only kids in our teens and weren't prepared for what seemed like bedlam at times.*

Debbie and the Darnels toured up and down the East Coast, and they were a very popular girl group in the early '60s. In Connecticut, Debbie and the Darnels performed in numerous music venues in the state such as *Connecticut Bandstand*, Seymour's Actors Colony and so on. They also shared the stage with other well-known Connecticut artists such as the Five Satins, the Passengers and New Haven's Ginny Arnell.

Songs by Debbie and the Darnels can be found on recent compilation CDs, such as *A Million Dollars Worth of Girl Groups* (released in 2000), *Christmas Doo-Wop & Pop Vol. 3* (released in 2013) and *Christmas Classics for Kids* (released in 2014).

Cookie and Charley

Cookie Teznick and Charley (Charlie) Lent were classmates at Hillhouse High School in New Haven. They were also popular regulars on the *Connecticut Bandstand* show in 1957. Later that year, Cookie and Charley recorded two singles (released in 1958): "Let's Go Rock and Roll" and "I Love You So." Lent cowrote both songs. The recordings were popular on a local basis, charting in the Top 20 on several Connecticut radio stations.

Ginny Arnell

Any of my records could be released and enjoyed today as well as they were sixty years ago. I believe my records are timeless and I'm so grateful that these recordings have been the source of enjoyment by so many people!
—Ginny Arnell

Ginny Arnell. *Courtesy of Ginny Arnell.*

Singer-songwriter Ginny Arnell was born Genevieve Mazzaro in New Haven. She lived on 40 Fair Street in New Haven until she was ten years old, at which time the family moved to East Haven. Ginny attended East Haven's Tuttle Elementary School and East Haven High School, class of 1960.

Genevieve began her professional career at the early age of eleven years old. She sang on New Haven's WELI as part of Youth on Parade and began singing at numerous music venues from then on.

Sixteen-year-old Genevieve began her recording career in earnest in 1957, when she teamed up with another singer to form the duo known as Jamie and Jane. Her singing partner (Jamie) was actually future Hall of Fame recording star Gene Pitney.

Jamie and Jane recorded several songs together. "Faithful Our Love" was cowritten by Pitney, Mazzaro and New Haven's Marty Kugell (a Connecticut producer who gained fame as producer of "In the Still of the Night" by the Five Satins). "Classical Rock and Roll" was written by Pitney. "Strolling (Thru the Park)" was cowritten by Mazarro (credited as Ginny Mazzaro).

The duo's songs charted locally and in various parts of the United States. (For example, "Snuggle Up Baby" charted No. 29 in Pittsburgh.) Jamie and Jane received favorable reviews in the July 29, 1957 edition of *Billboard* magazine, which gushed, "Material is imaginative…[and] the pair impress as new talent." The duo appeared in a number of Connecticut music venues, such as Bridgeport's Pleasure Beach in July 1959. Jamie and Jane had a very loyal fan club in the area.

Eventually, both Mazzaro and Pitney recorded as solo artists. Mazzaro's stage and recording name was changed to Ginny Arnell. Several well-known songwriters (Carole King, Neil Sedaka, Gerry Goffin, Teddy Randazzo, Jeff Barry and so on) penned some of her songs.

In 1963, Arnell recorded her highest-charting single, a tune called "Dumb Head." The song peaked at No. 50 on *Billboard*'s Top 100. Arnell performed this song on Dick Clark's *American Bandstand* TV show. She even re-recorded the tune in Japanese. "Dumb Head" fared even better in various U.S. radio markets (No. 3 on Chicago's WLS and Milwaukee's WRIT). In Connecticut, "Dumb Head" was a Top 10 hit (No. 8 on WAVZ). Arnell's "I Wish I Knew What Dress to Wear," recorded in 1964, appeared on *Billboard*'s chart as a "bubbling under" song.

Dorothy Yutenkas, of Debbie and the Darnels, reminisced about appearing with Ginny Arnell: "Ginny Arnell was an East Haven High School girl. Ginny and I competed in talent contests when we were very young. She has a very nice voice."

Ginny Arnell recalled a funny incident that happened to her as she was about to perform her song "Dumb Head" on Dick Clark's *American Bandstand* TV show:

> American Bandstand *was a highlight in my career. I was a big fan of the show. A funny thing happened when I was getting ready to lip sync the record. They put on a Bobby Rydell record, "Wild One," instead of "Dumb Head." So I stood there, smiled and waited for the producer to put on the right record. We all laughed about it and moved right along. I'll never forget it. I also recorded "Dumb Head" in Japanese where it was released and was a big hit.*

Ginny Arnell's "teenage pop sound" is reminiscent of such 1960s artists as Lesley Gore and Brenda Lee. One of her songs, "Look Who's Talkin'," appears on a 2013 CD titled *The Girl Group Sound: The Darlings of the 1960s, Volume 1*. Ginny Arnell toured nationwide. In Connecticut, she has shared the stage with other Connecticut artists such as Debbie and the Darnels and Danbury's the Hi-Lites. Arnell performed on the *Connecticut Bandstand* TV dance show on four occasions and also at record hops in Bridgeport and Fairfield.

By the time she appeared on *Connecticut Bandstand*, Ginny was a seasoned pro. Arnell recalled her experience on this show: "Performing on New Haven's *Connecticut Bandstand* TV show was a lot of fun. Jim Gallant [the host] was very nice and treated me like a professional, which I appreciated."

Art DeNicholas

A native of New Haven, Art DeNicholas has had a long and impressive career in the music business. Early on, DeNicholas was in a group called the Emeralds. He then cofounded a group with Tommy Juliano called the Hill Aces. (The section of New Haven where they lived was known as the Hill.) DeNicholas and Juliano were classmates at New Haven's Hillhouse High School.

In 1957, while still in school, DeNicholas and Juliano formed the Catalinas (aka the Buddies). At the end of 1963, DeNicholas and Juliano formed the Van Dykes (aka the Van Dyke Five) in New Haven. The group's music style was similar to the Four Seasons. The Van Dykes were extremely popular in the Connecticut area. They were the only Connecticut group to have three No. 1 songs in New Haven. The Van Dykes appeared on the same bill as the Shags and Fred Parris and the Restless Hearts in 1966 at the Teen Tempo '66 show in Milford. The group also performed at other Connecticut music venues, such as Seymour's Polynesian Room (1967).

Left: The Catalinas; *right*: The Van Dykes. *Both courtesy of Art DeNicholas (of the Van Dykes).*

Later on, DeNicholas became the manager of the 1960s West Haven band Bridge. Also, Art DeNicholas and Jerry Greenberg formed the Green Sea record label.

Andy Dio

When I was fourteen years old, I saw Andy Dio on Connecticut Bandstand. He performed his hit "Rough and Bold." Andy was fantastic, and the audience reaction was amazing! Soon after, I became the president of the Andy Dio fan club and continued to be a big fan of his music.
—Rose Marie DeGennaro DeMatteo

Andy Dio, Rose Marie DeGennaro De Matteo and DJ Dick Stephens (West Haven Record Hop). *Courtesy of Rose Marie DeGennaro De Matteo.*

Singer/songwriter Andy "Dio" Diotaiuto was a local legend in the New Haven area and even had a loyal and sizeable fan club. Rose Marie DeGennaro (De Matteo) was the national president of the Andy Dio fan club. Dio's songs were in the rockabilly and R&B music genre. His great recording "Rough and Bold" did not chart nationally, but it was a No. 1 song in New Haven in 1961. Dio was also an excellent trumpet player. In 1965, he had a solo trumpet part in the No. 2 *Billboard* smash hit "Lover's Concerto" by the Toys. He also toured with the Toys. In 1967, Dio backed up the Bob Crewe Generation on trumpet on the No. 15 *Billboard* hit "Music to Watch Girls By." In addition, Dio recorded and toured with Mitch Ryder and the Detroit Wheels.

Andy Dio also appeared on Jim Gallant's *Connecticut Bandstand* show, as well as the *Merv Griffin* and *Mike Douglas* TV shows.

The Pyramids

The Pyramids were an R&B vocal group that formed in New Haven in 1955. The teenage group backed New Haven's Ruby Whitaker in 1957 on her version of "I Don't Want to Set the World on Fire." They performed on Jim Gallant's *Connecticut Bandstand* TV show, singing "At Any Cost." The Pyramids were popular in the New Haven area.

Billy James

Billy James was born Bill Nosal in Glastonbury. Nosal was a 1963 graduate of Glastonbury High School (Hubbard Street, Glastonbury). In 1961, sixteen-year-old Billy James wrote and recorded "My Prayer." The song was released by Billy James and the Stenotones (aka Billy and the Stenotones). The record did very well on New England charts, staying on the charts for thirteen weeks and peaking at No. 2. The Stenotones consisted of several Connecticut female singers.

In 1962, "Meant for Me" and its B side "It's the Twist" were recorded by Billy James and the Crystal Tones. The Crystal Tones were a doo-wop vocal harmony group from New Britain.

James was also a member of the Connecticut band the Reveliers. In 1964, the Reveliers released the rocking instrumentals "Part III" and "Maureen." The band was led by Jerry Crane (guitar) and Billy James (organ). The Reveliers instrumentals were recorded at the Al Soyka Studios in Somers.

Billy James appeared on *Connecticut Bandstand* and *The Brad Davis Show* TV programs. In the '70s, James began using his real name (Bill Nosal) when he was an on-air radio personality for a few Connecticut radio stations and then program director for Hartford's WCCC radio station.

Jim Gallant Shows at Lake Compounce

> *Prior to going on stage for one of Jim Gallant's Lake Compounce shows in Bristol, Connecticut, the Premiers were in the dressing room practicing for the song "I Wonder Why." All of a sudden, the door opened and in walked four guys who stood there and watched us finish the song. One guy stepped forward and asked, "Are you guys planning on singing that song tonight?" My brother Roger Koob replied, "Yeah, why?" The other guy responded, "Well, that's our song." At first, we didn't recognize any of these guys. But it was Dion who asked the question. So, we all had a good laugh. The following Sunday, while the Premiers were walking up Broadway in NYC, we ran smack into the Belmonts. All the group members stopped, and we had a really nice conversation about music.*
>
> —*Bill Koob, of the Premiers*

Connecticut Bandstand disc jockey Jim Gallant hosted numerous record hops at Bristol's Lake Compounce. The record hops were known as the

Jim Gallant Lake Compounce Shows. The live record hops were first introduced by Gallant in 1957 and held on Thursday nights. To attract more high school students, the record hops were moved to Friday nights (8:00 p.m. to 11:00 p.m.) beginning May 15, 1958.

The record hop shows were popular teenager events and featured some well-known guest recording artists. These included Bobby Rydell performing "Kissing Time," Dion and the Belmonts and Johnny Tillotson, among others. Also featured were regional and local group favorites (such as the Premiers) and regulars from Jim Gallant's *Connecticut Bandstand* TV show.

4
THE BRAD DAVIS SHOW

TV DANCE PROGRAM

In May 1961, our song "She Gives Me Fever" reached No. 1 in New Haven and stayed that way for a while. On the strength of that song and a few other songs of ours that were popular in Connecticut, the Premiers were in demand constantly doing record hops all over Connecticut including record hops hosted by Biggie Nevins who took over as the host of Connecticut Bandstand. *Brad Davis reached out to us and we performed on his TV dance show. It was an exciting time for us.*
—*Bill Koob, member of the Premiers*

The *Brad Davis Show* TV dance program, sponsored by the Connecticut Milk Producers Association, premiered on Hartford's WTIC TV on October 3, 1959, and ran until 1969. The format was similar to *Connecticut Bandstand*, featuring teenagers who danced to the popular tunes at the time. The show featured regional musicians and national recording artists. Brad Davis hailed from Stafford Springs and graduated from Enfield High School.

The Brad Davis Show was broadcast on WTIC-TV from 4:30 p.m. to 5:00 p.m. every Saturday.

The following are some of the artists who performed on television's *Brad Davis Show*:

Historic Connecticut Music Venues

Left: Brad Davis. *Right*: Ad for appearances by Sly and the Family Stone and the Wildweeds on October 12, 1968. *Both author's collection.*

Sly and the Family Stone

Sly and the Family Stone performed on Brad Davis's TV dance show on October 12, 1968. Sly and his band were inducted into the Rock 'n' Roll Hall of Fame in 1993.

The Wildweeds

Windsor's Wildweeds appeared on *The Brad Davis Show* program on October 12, 1968. Also performing on the same show was Sly and the Family Stone.

Gene Pitney

Hall of Fame legend Gene Pitney appeared on *The Brad Davis Show* on numerous occasions. For example, Pitney performed his hit song "Town

Without Pity" on the December 23, 1967 program. Also featured on the same show was the singing group the Cowsills, who performed their hit "The Rain, The Park, and Other Things."

Frankie Valli

Frankie Valli and the Four Seasons have been one of the most prolific groups in rock 'n' roll history. They were one of the few American groups to withstand the onslaught of the British Invasion. According to their website, Frankie Valli and the Four Seasons had forty songs in the Top 40, nineteen in the Top 10 and eight No. 1 hits. They also had a Top 40 hit under their alias the Wonder Who. In addition, Frankie Valli had nine Top 40 hits as a solo artist. Valli was a guest on Hartford's *Brad Davis Show*.

The original members of the Four Seasons (Frankie Valli, Bob Gaudio, Nick Massi and Tommy DeVito) were inducted into the Rock 'n' Roll Hall of Fame in 1990. The Four Seasons were also inducted into the Vocal Group Hall of Fame in 1999.

Bridge

West Haven's Bridge was best known for local hits "It's a Beautiful Day" and "Love Is There." The song "Love Is There" was a No. 1 hit on local radio (WAVZ). Much of the band's original material was written by group members Dennis D'Amato and Charley Claude. Bridge recordings took place at Trod Nossel Studios.

The manager of Bridge was Art DeNicholas, the cofounder and group member of the bands the Van Dykes and the Catalinas. Bridge was popular in the New England region. The group (then known as the Symbolix) opened for the Young Rascals at the New Haven Arena. The band also performed on *The Brad Davis Show* program. Bridge broke up in 1971.

Tommy and the Rivieras

West Haven's Tommy and the Rivieras was one of the groups that appeared on the *The Brad Davis Show*. Fans may recall that Tommy and the Rivieras were the opening act for the Doors on December 9, 1967. During that

Historic Connecticut Music Venues

Left: Tommy and the Rivieras. *Author's collection*; *right*: The Premiers, *left to right*: Gus Delcos, Roger Koob and Frank Polemus, with Billy Koob in the front. *Courtesy of Bill Koob.*

concert, Jim Morrison of the Doors was arrested on stage and brought to the New Haven Police Department, where he was charged with obscenity and breach of peace.

The Blue Beats

The Blue Beats are probably best known for their rock song "Extra Girl," an extremely popular Top 10 song on Connecticut radio stations and at local dance clubs. Their follow-up recording "Born in Chicago" and its B side "I Can't Get Close (To Her at All)" were also well received in the Connecticut area.

The Blue Beats performed on the *The Brad Davis Show*. The band also performed as backup for major artists (Four Tops, Herman's Hermits at Bushnell Memorial, Hollies at Hartford's Armory and others).

The Blue Beats were a popular garage rock band that originated in Ridgefield. Band members hailed from the Ridgefield, Danbury and Westport areas. After the Blue Beats disbanded, several members reunited and joined a band called the No. 1.

Midnite Movers

The Midnite Movers were an R&B/soul band from Windsor. The group was founded by Ralph DeLorso Jr. in 1968. DeLorso was a 1972 graduate of Windsor High School. The Midnite Movers appeared on *The Brad Davis Show* in 1969. The band released six songs and recorded at Syncron Studio and studios in New Haven and Hartford. After touring throughout the Northeast, the Midnite Movers disbanded in 1971.

The Upbeats

The Upbeats hailed from Waterbury, and the band members graduated from Waterbury's Croft High School. In 1961, Jess Evon and Ralph Calabrese formed the Upbeats. The band members consisted of Jess Evon, Ralph Calabrese, Tom Nappi and Dave San Angel. The group backed numerous nationally known artists. The Upbeats performed on *The Brad Davis Show* in 1966.

The Marble Collection

New Haven's the Marble Collection appeared on *The Brad Davis Show* on two occasions.

5
THE GATHERING OF THE VIBES FESTIVAL

We played every Gathering of the Vibes festival since it began in 1997. GOTV definitely played a role in propelling Deep Banana Blackout's career and also the careers of other regional artists and bands. In the beginning, what was interesting to us was that our music was different than the more common jam scene at the time such as the Grateful Dead, Phish and other classic jam rock. We were a classic funk and soul act. But we discovered that the scene really needed that because it was a nice change of pace, still uplifting and fun, danceable and part of the GOTV history. We truly appreciate that we were so welcomed with that audience. Gathering of the Vibes really helped connect us to that large crowd.
—*Deep Banana Blackout band*

My favorite Gathering of the Vibes memory was in 1998. There was an end of night jam with all the bands who performed at GOTV for the four-day event that year. At one point, all of us on stage started jumping up and down like lunatics to the delight of the sea of people in attendance. All of a sudden, my pants started falling down to the point where my pants were down around my ankles. I was like, what am I freaking out about? It's all good! This cracked me up and stuck with me all these years as a constant reminder to not take things too seriously and to have fun with things like this. It reminds me of how cuckoo we all were. And the organizers did ask us back for the next year and all the years after that.
—*Fuzz (of Deep Banana Blackout)*

From the Coliseum to the Shaboo

The annual music festival known as the Gathering of the Vibes (GOTV) grew out of the need to fill the void that was left due to the death of Jerry Garcia of the Grateful Dead in 1995. Initially named "Deadhead Heaven—A Gathering of the Tribe" in 1996, the festival name was changed the following year to the "Gathering of the Vibes."

Seaside Park in Bridgeport has served as the host of the GOTV festival for eleven of the twenty years of the festival's existence. The GOTV festival was always well attended, attracting up to twenty-five thousand people each year for this four-day event. Wavy Gravy (of Woodstock fame) served as master of ceremonies for this festival from 2002 to 2015. Major world-class artists such as the Allman Brothers, CSN, James Brown, Bob Weir and Jaimoe's Jasssz Band performed at these events over the years. The festival also showcased many talented local bands in and around Connecticut.

Other notable artists who have performed at the Gathering of the Vibes:

Deep Banana Blackout

Deep Banana Blackout (DBB) grew out of a merger of two bands: Tongue and Groove and Pack of Matches. DBB formed in Connecticut's Fairfield County in 1995. Group members hailed from Bridgeport, Fairfield and New Haven. DBB boasts a wide variety of music genres, including funk, soul, rock, jam-rock and R&B. Between 1997 and 2011, Deep Banana Blackout performed ten times at Bridgeport's popular GOTV festival, as well as other Connecticut music venues, such as Toad's Place.

Left: Bob Weir (of the Grateful Dead). *Copyright Philamonjaro*; *right*: Deep Banana Blackout. *Courtesy of Fuzz, Deep Banana Blackout.*

HISTORIC CONNECTICUT MUSIC VENUES

Dr John

Dr John. *Copyright Philamonjaro.*

Dr John performed at the Gathering of the Vibes Festival on July 24–25, 2011. He also performed at other Connecticut music venues, including Waterbury's Municipal Stadium (September 28, 1972) and the Ridgefield Playhouse. Dr John was inducted into the Rock 'n' Roll Hall of Fame in 2011.

Rivers Cuomo (Weezer)

Singer, songwriter and guitarist Rivers Cuomo has a personal and musical connection to Connecticut. According to his bio, his mother named him after the East and Hudson Rivers near the Manhattan hospital where he was born. Soon after, the Cuomo family moved to an ashram farm in Pomfret, Connecticut (within a Hindu community referred to as Yogaville), and he attended Pomfret Community School on the ashram. The family later moved to Storrs-Mansfield (Connecticut), where Rivers attended Mansfield Middle School. While at Mansfield Middle School, Rivers went under the name Peter Kitts (named after his stepfather). In eighth grade (1984), Rivers and his schoolmate Justin Fisher decided to form their own band, which they called Fury. The band Fury consisted of Rivers (guitar, vocals), his brother Leaves Cuomo (rhythm guitar), Justin Fisher (bass) and Eric Robertson (drums). After rehearsing for a few months, Fury played its first gig in the fall of 1984. According to the website www.weezerpedia.com, the first song Rivers wrote was "Fight for Your Right," and an extract of a 1984 Fury rehearsal can be heard on the "I Wish You Had an Axe Guitar" track on the album *Alone: The Home Recordings of Rivers Cuomo*.

Rivers attended E.O. Smith High School (Storrs-Mansfield), class of 1988, under the name Peter Kitts. Rivers would later use E.O. Smith as the name of his music publishing company. In high school, Rivers had a role in his high school production of *Grease*, playing the part of Johnny Casino. At this time, Rivers and Justin formed the band Avant Garde (1985). Avant Garde consisted of Cuomo, Fisher, Michael Stanton, Kevin Ridel, Eric Ridel and Bryn Mutch. The band recorded their own songs, and they used the Cuomo house as their headquarters. For a time, Cuomo took guitar lessons from Jim Matheos of the Hartford band Fates Warning. According to weezerpedia.com, Stanton said that Rivers became a "rock star in the area."

In 1989, Rivers moved from Connecticut to Los Angeles along with Avant Garde, where he changed the name of the band to Zoom. Cuomo was involved in several other bands known as Fuzz and 60 Wrong Sausages. Rivers Cuomo eventually achieved international fame with his rock band Weezer (formed in 1992).

Weezer performed at Bridgeport's Gathering of the Vibes on August 2, 2015. Weezer also played at a number of other Connecticut music venues, including New Britain's the Sting, Toad's Place, Meadows Music Theatre, Bridgeport's Harbor Yard, Comcast Theatre, Foxwoods (three times) and Mohegan Sun.

Max Creek

Hartford's Max Creek (aka the Creek) is a jam rock band that was formed at the University of Hartford in 1971 by John Rider, Dave Reed and Bob Gosselin. The group was named after the small town in Virginia where Rider grew up. The band is known for its live improvisation performances.

In 1972, fifteen-year-old guitarist Scott Murawski joined Max Creek. Murawski is not only a great guitarist but also an accomplished drummer and pianist. It was Scott's involvement in the Creek that encouraged the band to change musical direction and move into the rock genre. Moreover, Murawski is the lead guitarist of Mike Gordon's band. (Gordon was the founder and bassist of the band Phish.) Max Creek had a great influence on Phish, and Gordon has regarded the Creek as one of his favorite bands.

The Creek was the recipient of the 2015 Connecticut Music Award for "Best Jamband." Max Creek has a very loyal fan base. Max Creek performed at the GOTV Festival in Bridgeport on eight occasions.

APPENDIX A
INTERVIEWS WITH TWO HALL OF FAME LEGENDS

Keith Richards Interview with *Goldmine*'s Patrick Prince (2021)

Note: Keith Richards has lived in Connecticut for well over twenty-five years.

Goldmine editor and Stratford resident Patrick Prince interviewed fellow Connecticut resident and Hall of Famer Keith Richards for the January 2021 issue of *Goldmine* magazine.

PATRICK PRINCE: It can now be seen as a blessing that in 1986 Mick Jagger made the decision not to go on tour to promote the latest Rolling Stones album, *Dirty Work*. Instead, Jagger chose to go into the studio to record a follow up to his debut solo effort, *She's the Boss*. Jagger's creative departure influenced guitarist Keith Richards to also make the decision to record his own material, releasing what is quite possibly the best Stones solo record to date, the fantastic *Talk Is Cheap*. Richards rounded up an extremely talented band to back him up in the studio and on tour, namely The X-Pensive Winos.

The Winos as a whole are a powerhouse band consisting of cream-of-the-crop session musicians and tour veterans: Waddy Wachtel, Ivan Neville, Charley Drayton, the late great saxophonist Bobby Keys and drummer Steve Jordan. Included in the mix was the very talented Sarah Dash. Proof

Appendix A

Keith Richards. *Left to right*: Ronnie Wood, Mick Taylor and Darryl Jones. *Copyright Philamonjaro.*

of the kind of performance this band could deliver was released on the 1991 CD *Live at the Hollywood Palladium, December 15, 1988*.

Here is Patrick's interview with Keith:

GOLDMINE: It feels like the perfect time to re-release this kind of live album. Most of us can't experience live shows because of the pandemic. People are missing the sound of the live experience.

KR: Yeah, it's strange. It's very difficult to talk about the pandemic, because, obviously, it set everybody into a spin, right? I expected to be working through the summer, as you know, and I did gardening instead.

GM: The extras are great in the Super Deluxe box set of this live album. They help the listener feel like they're almost at the show itself. I mean, the set is wrapped in a tour T-shirt, with replicas of a handwritten set list and ticket stubs…even the wine label and bag that you gave away at the show that night.

KR: I know. I'm very impressed with the record company guys who put my box sets together. And the *Talk Is Cheap* one was fantastic. I was listening back to the records and also working with Steve Jordan—I mean, we don't stop, (laughs) pandemic or not—and it was such a joy for us. And speaking to Waddy Wachtel at the time that we made these records, we were saying,

Appendix A

"Right now they're going to be appreciated. But I have a feeling there's going to be a lot more shelf life on these things." Weirdly enough, as a joke mostly then. And now to see them...and what beautiful packaging, man.

GM: And a 10-inch record comes with the set.

KR: Get that, vinyl freaks, all right!

GM: It has three previously unreleased songs on it, which is cool, especially "I Wanna Be Your Man." That song is almost better live than it was in the studio. Live it's like a rave-up, you know, with a lead break that is razor sharp. That's a great song to put on the 10-inch.

KR: Yeah, I couldn't resist playing it when we decided to play live. And I wanted to play that Beatles song, man! [laughs]

GM: Do you remember the last time you played that prior to this performance (and tour)? I think it was the mid-1960s.

KR: [laughs] I was hoping you could tell *me*, actually.

GM: I had to look it up—April 1965 in Albany, New York.

KR: We didn't do it a lot as the Stones, except when it came out in '64. I don't know why not, because it's great fun to play on stage. That's one of the reasons why I resurrected it for these shows. And it was such great fun for me. You know, it's enough you would think to be in one great band in your lifetime. And then suddenly realizing that growing up around you is another incredible unit. I learned so much from doing (the Winos). I needed it. I needed to do the Winos stuff in order to plow forward and go on with what Mick and I had to do. We needed that break and a fresh look at things, you know.

GM: Yeah, you even said after this Winos tour was done that you had a greater appreciation for Mick as a front man. You know, to lead a band... it's a lot of work.

KR: Absolutely. Absolutely, yes, because then I realized that I doubled the job up, right? By being the singer *and* the guitar player. Now I really get it!

GM: The song "Before They Make Me Run" was left off the original release of *Live at the Hollywood Palladium*. Was there a reason why you left a song like that off the record?

KR: I think it was a matter of running out of room. Because I love the song. I mean, I was probably forced at gunpoint to leave it off. [laughs]

GM: Out of all the shows that you played on this Winos tour, was there a reason why you picked the Palladium to record? Were other shows recorded?

KR: I had a feeling that it was probably because it was towards the end of the tour, I believe. And we figured that if we were going to record live you want to catch it while everyone's well into it. You don't want to record

Appendix A

the first show, you know. Also, I desperately wanted to have a live recording of this band, because at that time I didn't know if we'd get together again or what would happen. And I think a bit of luck was maybe involved. The Palladium's got a great sound.

GM: Yes, this album captures that intimacy of playing in a club. And that's got to be a high playing the clubs. I mean, I enjoy seeing a band like the Stones in an arena, but I prefer the clubs.

KR: Me too. It's that sort of re-magnified and reverberated energy in a small place that could really feed and stack things up.

GM: Let's go back to the band again. Waddy Wachtel nailed it when he said that this is the loosest tight band he's ever heard. That's a pretty accurate description of the Winos here.

KR: I think he nailed it, you're right. I can't think of a better one.

GM: It's tight, but it's organic sounding. And in popular music today, that organic sound is missed. Everything sounds so manufactured now.

KR: Should we use the real word? *Synthesized*. Are we allowed to say that still? [laughs] I mean, of course it is. And it blands everything out. And now on for a few years, I mean, your violins are a synthesizer, your drums are a synthesizer. How horrible, the idea of playing drums on a keyboard.

GM: And getting back to Waddy, that fuzz break that he does in "Take It So Hard"—he really added grit to that song.

KR: I think with Waddy, he just says give me a good song and I'll kill it. [laughs] He's played with everybody and everything.

GM: Do you think this (Winos lineup) was the best band that you've played with on a solo tour?

KR: As far as solo-wise, absolutely. Oh yeah, absolutely. As I said before, it has always astounded me, ever since working with the Winos who I've had a chance to work with. With the Stones you would think, that's enough already, you know. [laughs] Charlie Watts said something to me before I did anything solo. He said, if you think the occasion arises where you got to work outside of the Stones... he told me that Steve Jordan is my man. And I took Charlie at his word. And Steve and I (have) developed a relationship far beyond just his drumming or music or anything. And we got into the writing end of it and are still firm, firm friends. So I got so much out of working with the Winos, man. Like Ivan Neville (keyboards). Man, that guy has so much talent it's unbelievable. And Charley Drayton. I gotta mention Charley Drayton, an incredible bass player and drummer. And another thing I must say about the Winos, is that all of them are incredibly versatile. I could switch or they would switch themselves—only Waddy and I stayed with guitars, everybody

Appendix A

else was going "All right, I'll play the bass, you play the drums and we'll sort it out." I was amazed by the versatility of these men.

GM: And Sarah Dash! Geez, she can sing! And she said that she had a cold the night of the recording!

KR: Yes, unbelievable.

GM: You stated yourself that you didn't want to "Stones" up any of these songs, and you succeeded with her on "Time Is on My Side," because she brought it into different territory.

KR: It was always a lady's song to start with, with (singer) Irma Thomas. I have Sarah Dash and I have "Time Is on My Side"…Hey, I mean, I can take a hint. I'm going to put "Time Is on My Side" together with Sarah and let's go, you know…what an opportunity.

GM: How did you reconnect with her? The Stones toured with Patti LaBelle's group—which she was in—back in the 1960s.

KR: Yes, and that was about '65. And that was when Sarah was sort of allowed out of school to work with LaBelle's (group) over the summer holiday. So that's when we met. She was called "Inch" then. And I never forgot her. And then her name cropped up—I think via Steve Jordan. While we started putting together the Winos, he said, "We're going to need a female, you know, boys," and Sarah Dash came up, and what an incredible lady and what a voice.

GM: She was definitely a blessing on this live album and, like I said, the band was so tight, and then you had her…it was like the perfect element.

KR: Yeah, exactly. The golden opportunity. It was like you've been handed this stuff on a plate, you know. [laughs] Hey, the next life's gonna be awful!

GM: So this Palladium album is released for the first time on vinyl. And you're a record collector. Are you surprised on this resurgence of vinyl records as a format?

KR: No, I'm not surprised. At the same time, I'm very encouraged, because I always thought that people that know their sound, that really know it, they're not going to be fobbed off with these digital synthesizers forever. They'll listen to it and then there's going to be a resurgence of vinyl. And I thought this 20 years ago. I'm so happy to see the resurgence of vinyl, because I knew there's millions of people out there that do have really good ears and know what true sound is.

GM: Right. And, you know, if I downloaded or streamed the new live album, I might not know things like it's Sarah Dash singing on a song like "Time Is on My Side." With liner notes on an album, you get all that information.

Appendix A

KR: I know. Let's face it. Everybody's been sold second-hand goods—I mean, in order to sell things more and blah, blah, blah. The usual reasons, like greed. But there will be discerning people that know what's what, and apparently there's more and more. So it's very encouraging.

GM: And since most *Goldmine* readers are record collectors, they know you're a big supporter of the format, and recorded history, especially the blues. But some might not know that you are even on the Board of Advisors for the Archive of Contemporary Music (ARC), and you've curated their entire blues record collection. How did you get involved with that?

KR: Because you talk to me and it's about the blues and vinyl and I'm in. It's like you don't even have to question me. I'm so glad that vinyl is alive and kicking, because I can't listen to this trash no more, listening to people trying to play drums on a keyboard.

GM: It's great that you are trying to preserve something that was almost lost—a lot of these things were almost lost to history. A lot of these old records.

KR: It's amazing. I mean a lot of the things that are sort of taken for granted…it's the way we are. We're called the human race and [laughs] I don't know what the rush is.

GM: Record Store Day has really helped record stores and it's helped bring the vinyl format back to the mainstream. You've been involved with some great Record Store Day releases—you had "Run Rudolph Run" and [in 2020] you've released a red vinyl 7-inch single in 2020 "Hate It When You Leave" with the B-side "Key to the Highway" [which only saw release on the Japanese version of the album *Main Offender*]. You've been busy.

KR: "Key to the Highway," yes, that was another buried classic with (pianist) Johnnie Johnson that came out on Saturday the 24th of October 2020. I'm doing a blitz, you see. [laughs]

GM: Do you still get a chance to go to record stores?

KR: Very rarely, especially this year. Over the course of time…yeah, I do like to peek in. It's the browsing, right? Have a look. See who's got what and, of course, most record stores if they still exist these days are sort of a specialty in one kind of music or another, so…I'm just hoping everybody can survive through this crap.

GM: Hope to see this Winos crew get together again. I mean, if it were normal times, maybe you tour behind this Winos record, this rerelease, you know?

KR: I'll drink to that!

Appendix A

Felix Cavaliere Interview with *Goldmine* (2018)

NOTE: Felix Cavaliere lived in Connecticut for over seventeen years.

Goldmine: In 2014, after your outdoor concert, we talked about the flip side of "You Better Run," the crowd favorite "Love Is a Beautiful Thing." You told me, "We had plenty of time in the studio in the spring of 1966, working on our second album *Collections*." You stated, "We wrote 'Love Is a Beautiful Thing' there. It all just came together." Anything else about that experience?

FC: We had free studio time. When Atlantic had first approached us to join the label, we said that we wanted to produce ourselves and they allowed us that freedom. We were in charge. We played all the time in the studio. With "Love Is a Beautiful Thing," I had started the song and the other guys played their parts to build it up. We were truly a band. I'll tell you another flip side story. We always tried to put a really good song on our flip sides, hoping that the DJs would play that one too, like they would with The Beatles. For "Good Lovin'," which was a No. 1 selling single, we had our version of "Mustang Sally" on its flip side. Many years later, after a concert, a guy came up to me with a hug and kiss, saying that I helped to change his life. It was Mack Rice, who wrote "Mustang Sally." I guess between Wilson Pickett and our band we did change his life with our 1966 version.

GM: I bought a pair of Rascals singles with picture sleeves in 1968, as soon as they were released. The year began peacefully with "A Beautiful Morning" and by summer the country was very ready for your anthem "People Got to Be Free."

FC: "A Beautiful Morning" does start off peacefully with wind chimes. I was inspired by the opening of The Beatles' "Yellow Submarine." I thought it was a cool idea where they established a sound picture with an aquatic vision. I told that to Paul McCartney years later, too. With the sound effects and studio time, we were like kids in a candy store (called Atlantic Records). That label, though, wasn't too thrilled initially with "People Got to Be Free." They didn't want to get involved in any controversy. I had volunteered, supporting Bobby Kennedy's candidacy. Martin Luther King was assassinated earlier in the year and I was away in Jamaica. I got the news on short wave radio of Bobby's assassination and knew that I had to do something. When the label was reluctant to release the single, we demanded that it come out. I am so proud that it went to No. 1 and that the song was well received in oppressed cities not only in the U.S., but also oppressed places worldwide, including Hong Kong, South Africa and Berlin.

Appendix A

GM: In 1979, when your *Castles in the Air* album was released, my wife Donna and I married in our hometown of Cleveland, and early in the following year we moved across the country and only knew people from work. When your single from the album, "Only a Lonely Heart Sees," entered Top 40 radio, it felt like a reunion with an old friend. Your music has entertained my family for so many years.

FC: When a group breaks up, like The Rascals did in the 1970s, it is really hard. Very few survive. Paul McCartney and a few others are among the exceptions. I was pleased when "Only a Lonely Heart Sees" became a Top 40 hit and I was thrilled when I heard that the song was a #14 hit in Connecticut, where I lived for over 17 years. The song also reached No. 2 on the adult contemporary charts.

FC: Thank you, my man for our time together. I appreciate your good words.

APPENDIX B

THE AMAZING AND MYSTERIOUS SAGA OF THE MEGA-HIT SONG "(NA NA HEY HEY) KISS HIM GOODBYE" RECORDED BY A BRIDGEPORT TRIO

I had the great privilege of recording and touring with Gary DeCarlo. I actually backed Gary for the second and third remake recording of his huge hit "(Na Na Hey Hey) Kiss Him Goodbye." The last time I saw Gary was when I was on tour with Vincent Ingala and did a gig in Prospect, Connecticut. Gary came out to see us and we asked Gary to come up on stage to sing Na Na with us. The audience loved it and sang along. Such a wonderful memory! When I heard that he had passed, I had a hole in my heart.
Gary DeCarlo was a wonderful person, a talented singer, and had a gift that made people happy!
—Al Ferrante, musician

The No.1 smash hit "(Na Na Hey Hey) Kiss Him Goodbye" by a band known as Steam has a strange, legendary and almost mythical history to it. The story behind the band Steam is also somewhat complicated and mysterious.

The song can be traced back to 1961, when three Bridgeport, Connecticut teenagers cowrote a song they called "Kiss Him Goodbye." The song was not recorded and never released. The three teenagers were Gary DeCarlo, Dale Frashuer and Paul Leka. All three attended high schools in Bridgeport—Leka (Bassick High), DeCarlo (Central High) and Frashuer (Roger Ludlowe High). Soon after, DeCarlo and Frashuer joined a group known as the Glenwoods. The other members of that group were Joe Reed, Johnny Castle (Castlelenetti) and Frank Borelli. The group's name

Appendix B

changed several times, first to the Citations and then to the Chateaus. Leka sat in with the groups and played piano. DeCarlo described the original version of the song as "a blues shuffle." After the Chateaus broke up, Leka, DeCarlo and Frashuer went their separate ways.

In 1969, Leka, DeCarlo and Frashuer got together again. At this time, Leka was producing records for DeCarlo, who used the stage name Garrett Scott.

As fate would have it, this author was the last person to interview DeCarlo, not knowing the extent of Gary's illness (DeCarlo passed away several months later in Branford, Connecticut). During the interview, DeCarlo said he wanted to "set the record straight" and described the making of "(Na Na Hey Hey) Kiss Him Goodbye":

> I had cut four songs for Mercury records which Paul (Leka) and the executives felt were all great songs. Paul's favorite was "Workin' on a Groovy Thing" (written by Neil Sedaka). However, the Fifth Dimension found out about this recording and put their version out one week before mine. The record executives and Paul then decided to put out the ballad "Sweet Laura Lee" (written by Larry Weiss). I wasn't too keen on leading off with a ballad but was assured that it would be promoted to everyone's satisfaction. So now we needed a B side. I always liked the song "Kiss Him Goodbye" that we wrote years before. So I told Dale to tell Paul I wanted to record it. When we went into the studio, Paul pulled up one of the four songs that I had worked on which was called "Sugar" (also written by Neil Sedaka). Hearing this song again, we made an eight-bar drum loop that became the drum track. We also used piano and organ overdubs as well as vibes—but no bass and no guitar. At one point, I noticed a piece of wood on the floor from one of the organ speakers in the studio, so I picked up a pair of drumsticks and began playing rhythm on this board. Paul said "Hey, let's include this in the recording." So, I put cloth around the tips of the drumsticks while Paul held the board up to the microphone, and that became the rhythm percussion that you hear on the song. I sang the lead on the song. Needing a chorus for the song, Paul began using "na na's" instead of real words. I added the "hey" chants. The recording took a fortuitous turn when a record executive decided to release the song separately as an A-side. Somewhat mysteriously, a fictitious group name was shown as the recording artist, instead of "Garrett Scott," which allegedly was the original plan. (Garrett Scott was my stage name at the time.) I was told by Paul that when both records were released they would both be mine, but that did not happen.

Appendix B

Gary DeCarlo and Al Ferrante. *Courtesy of Al Ferrante.*

Soon the song began to be played in one sports venue after another. The fans and the public embraced the song, especially the chanting chorus. "(Na Na Hey Hey) Kiss Him Goodbye" became a monster No. 1 hit, with estimated sales of over seven million copies worldwide and counting. The song remained at No. 1 for two weeks, spending sixteen weeks on *Billboard*'s Hot 100 singles chart in 1969. It was also an international smash hit.

So now the trio had a major hit record but no band to promote the hit song. For a group, six Connecticut musicians were chosen to tour as the band and were given the group name Steam. According to DeCarlo, "Steam got its name when Paul, Dale and I were returning from lunch one day and we noticed steam shooting up from a NYC manhole."

Also, it was decided that a Steam album should be recorded, featuring their hit song. But who would sing on the album? As DeCarlo recalled, "Paul wanted me to sing all the songs on the album but have the tour group that was hired get the song credits. Of course I said no, and that, unfortunately, led to a rift in our friendship and business relationship. The tour band came from the Bridgeport area."

The Steam tour band appeared on various TV shows, most notably Dick Clark's *American Bandstand*. Clark displayed Steam's gold record on his podium during the band's performance. This was upsetting to DeCarlo

Appendix B

since the Steam band had nothing to do with this song. As the lead singer and co-writer of this hit song, DeCarlo felt he never received proper credit.

On August 25, 2016, Gary released a CD called *Now and Then* under his real name, Gary DeCarlo. He rerecorded and released a new version of "(Na Na Hey Hey) Kiss Him Goodbye" on his 2014 album *Long Time Comin'*.

"(Na Na Hey Hey) Kiss Him Goodbye" has been covered by many other artists over the years, including Bananarama (No. 5 in the United Kingdom in 1983) and the Nylons (No. 12 in 1987).

The Steam Tour Band

The Steam tour band appeared on *American Bandstand* on Saturday, December 27, 1969 (the thirteenth season of *American Bandstand*). As noted, the group known as Steam did not record the mega-hit "(Na Na Hey Hey) Kiss Him Goodbye." The song was actually recorded by the Bridgeport, Connecticut trio Gary DeCarlo, Paul Leka and Dale Frashuer. Six musicians from Bridgeport were selected to go on tour under the group name Steam and perform this hit song on *American Bandstand* and other music venues.

Paul Leka

Paul Leka had a mansion in Sharon, Connecticut. What a grand old place that was! Paul had just bought the place and seemed to always be out mowing the lawn! It was empty of furniture, but those mansions didn't need any. They just needed bands and music, jokes and laughter, and there was plenty of that. It was a great place to practice and rehearse, and then head to his recording studio in Bridgeport, Connecticut when it was time to record. The Maggie Band was one of the bands that rehearsed at Paul's mansion.
—*Linda Sunderland, wife of Maggie Band's Ed Sunderland*

I was living in Danbury and would drive to Bridgeport to play and record with some of the local guys there. This was in the mid-1970s. Bridgeport's Paul Leka owned the Connecticut Recording Studio and was well known in the area. I needed a guitarist right away, and Leka mentioned this guy, Vinnie Cusano, from Bridgeport. The kid came into the studio and was unbelievable! He really, really had talent. After having him play on a couple

Appendix B

of sessions, I had an idea. I said, "Hey, why don't we do an album?" And so we formed a band called Treasure and recorded some tracks on an album at Paul Leka's studio. Vinnie Cusano eventually changed his name to Vinnie Vincent and achieved fame as a member of Kiss. Also performing on the album was the very fine drummer Jack Scarangella.

—*Felix Cavaliere*

Connecticut has played a prominent role in both the personal and professional life of Paul Leka. After all, he was born and raised here, made his home here, married here, worked at a manufacturing company here, began his songwriting and had a vocal group career here, owned a recording studio here and, at the end, was buried here.

Born and raised in Bridgeport, Connecticut, Paul Leka became proficient in piano at an early age, with a concentration on classics. He soon learned to play multiple instruments, which would serve him well later in his career.

Leka attended Bridgeport's Bassick High School. In 1961, while still a student at Bassick High, Leka and two other high school friends wrote a song they called "Kiss Him Goodbye." The song was not recorded and never released. The three teenage songwriters were Gary DeCarlo, Dale Frashuer and Paul Leka. In a twist of fate, this song would reemerge eight years later and become a No. 1 smash hit record.

Paul worked for a time as an expediter at Avco Lycoming Manufacturing in Stratford. In 1964, Leka married his first wife, Rosemary Angela Gajnos. The marriage ceremony took place in St. Raphael's Church in Bridgeport. In addition, Leka was in the wedding party for his friend and Chateaus co-founder Dale Frashuer. The wedding also took place in Bridgeport.

Leka eventually decided to concentrate on songwriting and on the arranging and producing side of the music business. In 1966, Leka composed "Falling Sugar," which was recorded by the pop-rock band the Palace Guard. The song fared well in several markets (Top 20 on KUTY in Palmdale, California). Note: one of the group members of the Palace Guard was Don Grady (aka Don Agrati), who later starred as Robbie Douglas on the *My Three Sons* TV show.

Paul Leka is probably best known for his association with the groups Steam and the Lemon Pipers. Leka cowrote and produced the million-dollar seller and No. 1 *Billboard* hit "Green Tambourine" for the Lemon Pipers. In 1969, Leka (along with DeCarlo and Frashuer) took their 1961 song "Kiss Him Goodbye" and turned it into the No. 1 monster hit "(Na Na Hey Hey) Kiss Him Goodbye."

Appendix B

Paul Leka opened his own recording studio, Connecticut Recording Studio, on Main Street in Bridgeport. He produced and arranged for many major recording artists, including REO Speedwagon, Felix Cavaliere, Harry Chapin, the Left Banke, Steam, the Maggie Band and others. In 1975 and 1976, Leka arranged songs at his studio for the soul/funk group Black Satin featuring Fred Parris. Paul Leka died at age sixty-eight on October 12, 2011. He was buried in Sharon, Connecticut.

The Maggie Band

The Maggie Band was a 1970s Connecticut group, originally called Niagra Maggie. Their name was subsequently changed to the Maggie Band. The band's leader, Ed Sunderland, hails from Glastonbury. Members of the Maggie Band were Ed Sunderland (guitar, vocals), Steve Roy (bass), Kent Barbour (keyboards), Gerry Lark (sax) and Teed Donnelly (drums)

The Maggie Band played in a number of small music venues in Connecticut and were the opening act for artists such as Patti Smith.

At one point, the Maggie Band was a protege of Paul Leka. The band rehearsed in Leka's mansion in Sharon, Connecticut, and recorded at Paul Leka's recording studio in Bridgeport, Connecticut (known as the Connecticut Recording Studio).

The Maggie Band relaxing at Paul Leka's Recording Studio. *Back row, left to right*: Ron Bacchiocchi, Steve Roy, Ed Sunderland and Kent Barbour; *front row, left to right*: Gerry Lark, Teed Donnelly and Paul Leka (producer). *Courtesy of Linda Sunderland.*

APPENDIX C
BEHIND-THE-SCENES PHOTOS OF ARTISTS (INCLUDING SOME RARE PHOTOS)

A live concert to me is exciting because of all the electricity that is generated in the crowd and on stage. It's my favorite part of the business, live concerts
—*Elvis Presley*

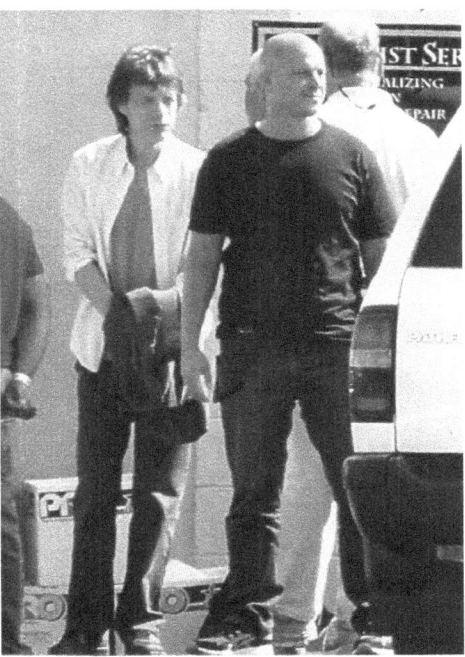

Mick Jagger at rehearsal. *Copyright Ivor Levene.*

Appendix C

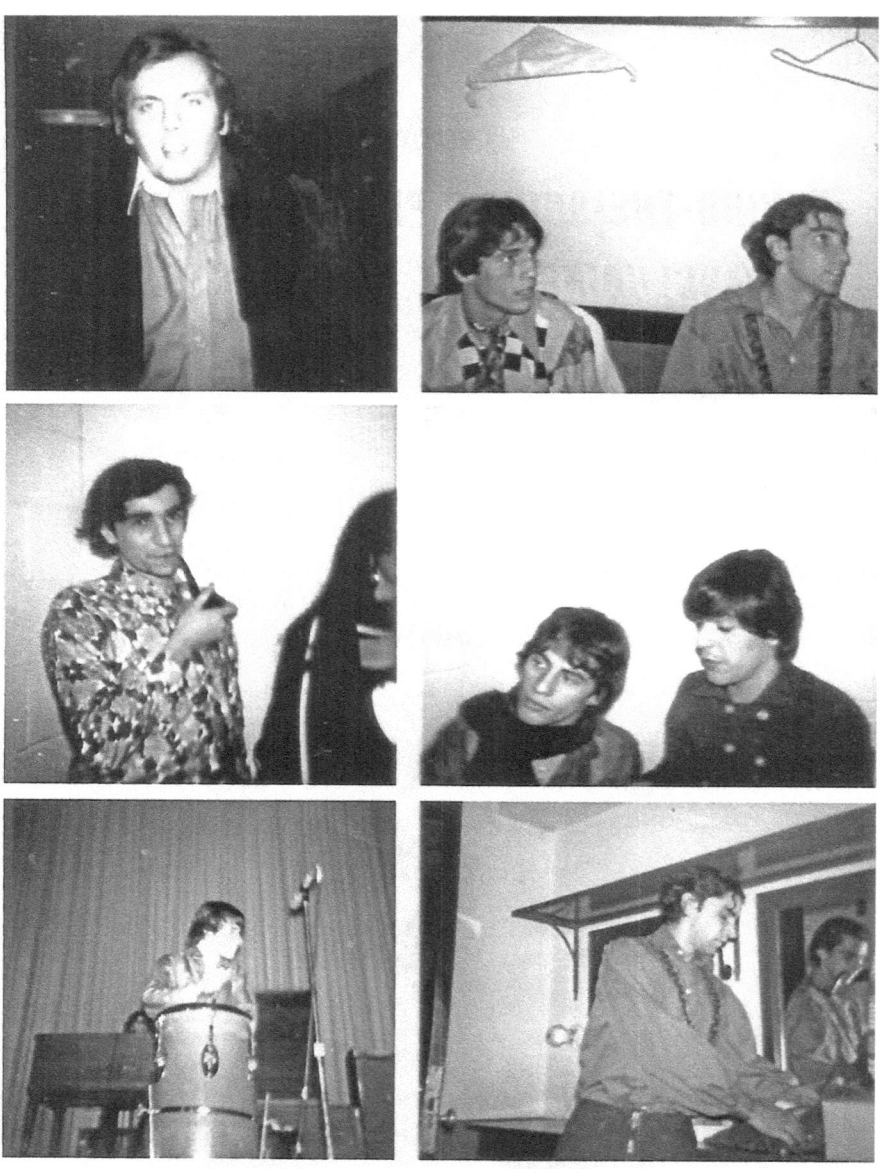

The Rascals, *clockwise from top left*: The Rascals' Gene Cornish backstage after Staples High concert, 1967; the Rascals' Eddie (*left*) and Felix at the Sandhaus home, 1967; the Rascals' Eddie (*left*) and Dino at the Sandhaus home, 1967; the Rascals' Felix Cavaliere backstage after Staples High concert, 1967; the Rascals on stage at Westport's Staples High, 1967; Felix Cavaliere with his pipe relaxing after concert at the Sandhaus home, 1967. *Copyright Ellen Sandhaus.*

Appendix C

Jimi Hendrix backstage at the Bushnell Memorial with Jeanette Jacobs (of the Cake and Ginger Baker's Air Force), 1968. *Courtesy of Henry McNulty.*

Appendix C

A rare photo of Eric Clapton taken during a Roger Waters show in 1985. Roger had asked Eric to be "his guitarist." Clapton only played a few shows before leaving the tour. Note that Clapton is wearing headphones, which allowed him to follow the strict format of the music. *Copyright Ivor Levene.*

Appendix C

Jeff Beck. *Copyright Ivor Levene.*

Left: Christine Ohlman and James Cotton. *Courtesy of Christine Ohlman*; *right*: Ronnie Spector (of the Ronettes) with Scott Spray, 1990. *Courtesy of Scott Spray.*

APPENDIX C

The Music Explosion, *left to right*: Burton Stahl, Bobby Avery, Jamie Lyons, Don (Tudor) Atkins, Rick Nesta. *Courtesy of Burton Stahl.*

Left: The Fifth Estate on tour, hot dogs for breakfast at 3:00 a.m. *Right*: On the tour bus leaving the Bushnell Memorial show, 1967. *Front row*, *left to right*: Rick Nesta (Music Explosion) and George Young (Easybeats); *second row*: Bill Shute (Fifth Estate); *third row*: Jamie Lyons (Music Explosion). *All courtesy of Ken Evans (of the Fifth Estate).*

Appendix C

Left: Peter Noone after Oakdale performance (summer 1968); *right*: The Left Banke, backstage at the West Hartford Armory, 1968. *Courtesy of Henry McNulty.*

Fred Parris with Charles Rosenay. *Courtesy of Charles Rosenay.*

Appendix C

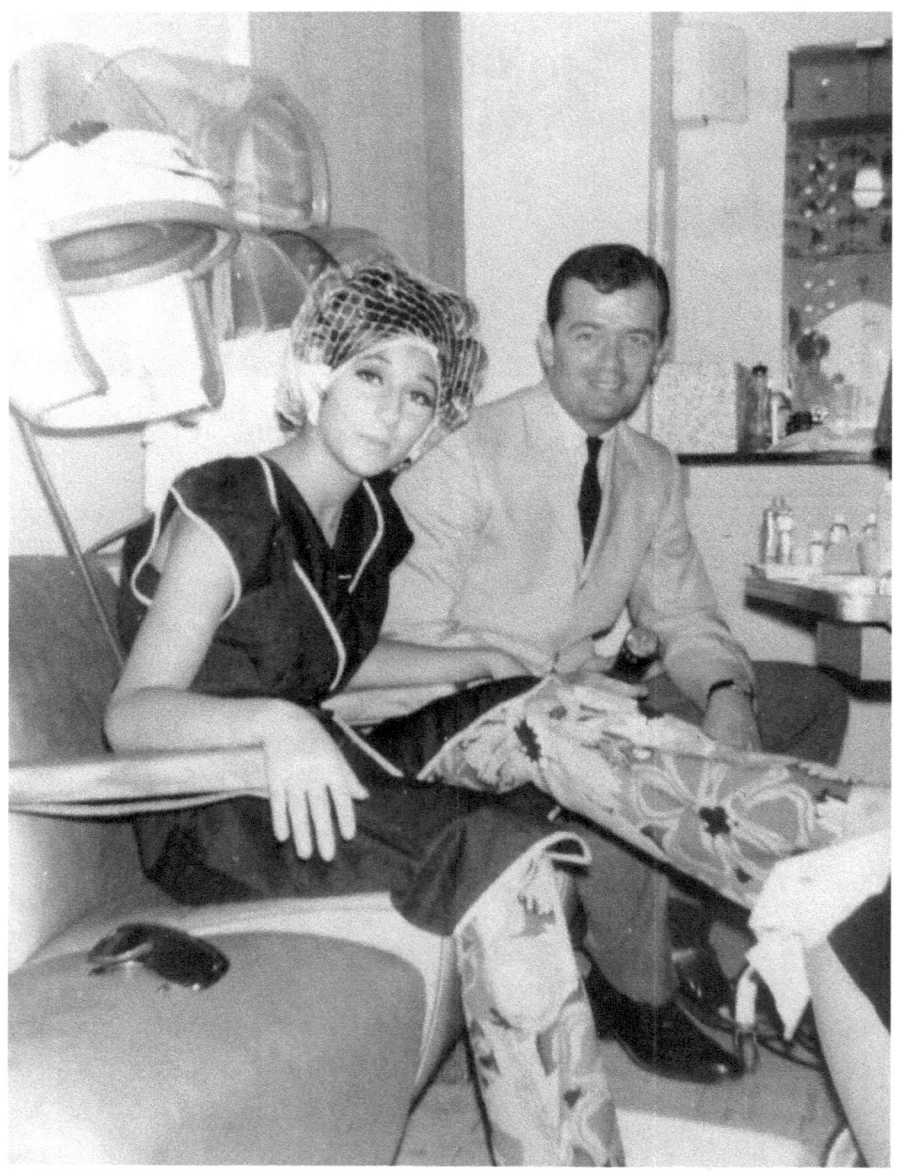

Cher with WDRC DJ Dick Robinson in Hartford, Connecticut. *Courtesy of Robinson Entertainment, LLC.*

Appendix C

Left: Michael Bolton (with Charles Rosenay). *Courtesy of Charles Rosenay, producer*; *right*: The Bridge. *Courtesy of Dennis D'Amato (of Bridge)*.

Huey Lewis after his concert in Hamden, Connecticut. *Courtesy of Marilyn Hewitt*.

Appendix C

Rare photo of Gene Pitney prior to his concert in Bournemouth, England. *Courtesy of Brian Dench.*

Appendix C

The original Alice Cooper band. *Left to right*: Neal Smith, Michael Bruce, Alice Cooper and Dennis Dunaway (cofounder). *Copyright Len DeLessio.*

BIBLIOGRAPHY

Balzano, Nicholas. *The Sultans Chronicles: Stories of One American Band*. Self-published, 2020.

Dunaway, Dennis. *Snakes! Guillotines! Electric Chairs!: My Adventures in the Alice Cooper Group*. New York: St. Martin's Griffin, 2018.

Gargan, Scott. "Born and Raised: 10 Things You May Not Know about John Mayer." *Connecticut Post*, December 10, 2013.

Schmidt, Randy L. *Little Girl Blue*. London: Music Sales, 2012.

Staudter, Thomas. "Connecticut at Its Best: Where the Music That 'Opens Your Soul' Has a Home." *New York Times*, December 12, 2004. https://www.nytimes.com/2004/12/12/nyregion/connecticut-at-its-best-where-the-music-that-opens-your-soul-has-a.html.

Steinberg, Brian. "The Attraction of Toad's." *Yale Alumni* magazine, Devember 1993. http://archives.yalealumnimagazine.com/issues/93_12/toads.html.

Websites

AZ Quotes | www.azquotes.com
Better Cheaper Slower | www.bettercheaperslower.com
Brainy Quote | www.brainyquote.com
Branford Historical Society | www.branfordhistoricalsociety.org
Brave Words | www.bravewords.com

Bibliography

Cinema Treasures. "State Theatre: Main Street and Morgan Street, Hartford, CT." www.cinematreasures.org/theaters/1960.
Connecticut Post | www.ctpost.com
CT Insider | www.shorelinetimes.com
Dennis Dunaway | www.dennisdunaway.com
Eight to the Bar | www.eighttothebar.com
FAB4 Music Festival | www.Fab4MusicFestival.com
Felix Cavaliere's Rascals | www.felixcavalieremusic.com
The Fifth Estate | www.thefifthestateband.com
Frankie Valli and the Four Seasons | www.frankievallifourseasons.com
Gathering of the Vibes Festival | www.gatheringofthevibes.com
Goldmine | www.goldminemag.com
Goodreads | www.goodreads.com/quotes
Hartford Courant | www.courant.com
Hartford Healthcare Amphitheatre | www.hartfordhealthcareamp.com
International Beatleweek Festival | www.LiverpoolTours.com
Len DeLessio | www.delessio.com
Levitt Pavilion for the Performing Arts | www.levittpavilion.com
Mansion Road Music | www.mansionroadmusic.com
New Haven Museum | www.newhavenmuseum.org
New Haven Register | www.nhregister.com
Newspapers | www.newspapers.com
New York Times | www.nytimes.com
The Official Home of Christine Ohlman | www.christineohlman.net
Patch | www.patch.com
Philamonjaro | www.philamonjaro.com
Rock & Roll Hall of Fame | www.rockhall.com
Rolling Stone | www.rollingstone.com
Ronnie Spector and the Ronettes | www.ronniespector.com
Toyota Oakdale Theatre | www.oakdale.com
Weezerpedia | www.weezerpedia.com

INDEX

A

Academics, the 37, 72, 129, 130, 133, 134
Actors Colony, music venue 31, 37, 42, 64, 73, 74, 75, 136
Aerosmith band 52, 118
Alcatrazz band 27, 28, 29, 115
Alice Cooper 24, 25, 26, 95, 106, 107, 127, 177
Amann, Charles, American Bandstand historian 131, 133
American Bandstand, TV show 42, 69, 130, 131, 132, 133, 138, 163, 164
"American Pie" 35
American Shakespeare Theatre, music venue 87, 88
Anderson, "Big Al" 12, 50, 52, 57, 60, 61, 91, 92, 93, 94, 96, 101
Arnell, Ginny 40, 41, 75, 130, 136, 137, 138

B

Baker, Ginger 20, 169
Beach Boys, the 38, 90, 115, 127
Beck, Jeff 90, 118, 171
"Beep Beep" 73, 74
"Be My Baby" 116
Berry, Chuck 30, 34, 35, 38, 76, 115, 123
"Black on White" 69
Blake Street Gut Band 114
Blue Beats, band 146
Blue Coupe, the 26, 107, 119
Blue Oyster Cult 97, 107
Bolton, Michael 49, 111, 112
Bono 27
Bouchard Brothers 26, 97, 107
Brad Davis Show, The 16, 37, 141, 143, 144, 145, 146, 147
Bram Rigg Set, band 49, 61, 67, 104, 113
Bridge 145
Buckinghams, the 38, 44

INDEX

Burr, Gary 86
Bushnell Memorial 35, 38, 39, 40, 42, 44, 57, 88, 124, 146, 169, 172

C

Cafe 9, music venue 91, 96
Carpenters, the 100, 101
Catalinas, the 130, 139, 145
Cavaliere, Felix 12, 17, 21, 50, 51, 88, 98, 99, 115, 116, 117, 119, 120, 127, 159, 165, 166
Cher 174
Cheri Shack, the 61, 65, 66, 67, 68, 69, 93
Clapton, Eric 78, 86, 115, 122, 170
Clark, Dick 130, 131, 133, 138, 163
Clarkson, Kelly 86, 104
Como, Perry 29, 105
Connecticut Bandstand, TV show 16, 37, 129, 130, 131, 132, 133, 134, 135, 136, 137, 139, 140, 141, 142, 143
Cookie and Charley, *Connecticut Bandstand* regulars 130, 137
Cream 20, 86
Crow, Sheryl 124
Cuomo, Rivers, Weezer 53, 150, 151

D

Daltry, Roger 26
Davies, Debbie 112
Davis, Brad 143
Debbie and the Darnels 31, 74, 130, 135, 136, 139

DeCarlo, Gary 161, 164, 165
Deep Banana Blackout, the 148, 149
DeNicholas, Art 139, 140, 145
Derringer, Rick 51, 103, 106
Dillon Stadium 84, 89, 90
"Ding Dong! The Witch Is Dead" 46
Dio, Andy 130, 140
Dion 30, 41, 49, 141, 142
D-Men, the 44, 45, 46, 47, 114
Dolenz, Micky 128
Doors, the 16, 19, 61, 90, 100, 145, 146
Doo-Wop 31, 32, 36, 38, 40, 141
Dr John 150
"Dumb Head" 138
Dunaway, Dennis 24, 25, 106, 107, 177
Dylan, Bob 38, 69, 70, 71, 79, 106, 120

E

Easybeats, the 44, 172
Eight to the Bar, ETTB 106, 110
Evans, Ken 38, 44, 45, 46, 47, 48, 96, 172

F

Faces, band 90
Feliciano, Jose 51
Fifth Estate band 38, 44, 45, 46, 47, 48, 61, 96, 114, 172
Fisher, Dave 72, 134
Five Satins, the 17, 30, 31, 32, 49, 74, 136, 137
Flares, the 59, 62, 63

182

Flying Tigers, the 106, 107
Foster, David "Lefty" 50, 51
Foxwoods Theatre 16, 35, 42, 43, 58, 79, 80, 104, 109, 117, 123, 124, 125, 126, 151
Freed, Alan 30, 33, 34, 38, 47, 81, 130

G

Gallant, Jim, *Connecticut Bandstand* 129, 130, 131, 134, 139, 140, 141, 142
Ganter, Marty 129, 133, 134
Gathering of the Vibes, festival 148, 149, 150, 151
Gene Pitney Show, the 38, 43, 44, 47
Goldmine 153, 158

H

Haley, Bill 34
Happenings, the 38, 44, 63
Hardknox, band 112
Hartford Civic Center, the 16, 27, 35, 79, 80, 83, 84, 85, 86, 104, 105, 114, 121, 124
Hartford HealthCare Amphitheater, the 126, 127
Hartford State Theatre 29, 30, 31, 34, 35, 37, 38
Havens, Richie 51, 76, 128
Heart, band 78, 80
Hendrix, Jimi 39, 53, 55, 56, 74, 122, 169
Herman's Hermits, the 102, 146
"He's a Rebel" 41, 42

Highwaymen folk group, the 48, 69, 70, 72, 73, 134
Holly, Buddy 30, 34, 35
Hullabaloo, music venue 45, 46, 47, 63, 64

I

"I'm Gonna Be Strong" 38, 42, 43
Indian Neck Folk Festival 69, 70, 71, 72, 73
Infinity Hall, music venue 116, 118, 119, 120, 125
"In the Still of the Night" 31, 32, 137

J

Jagger, Mick 84, 108, 153, 167
James, Billy, Nosal 130, 141
Jamie and Jane. *See* Gene Pitney 40, 41, 75, 137, 138
Jasper Wrath, band 58
Joel, Billy 38, 86, 109
John, Elton 18, 86, 115, 120
Johnson, Jack 121
Joplin, Janis 38, 76, 78

K

Keys, Alicia 103
Koob, Bill 17, 29, 30, 37, 40, 81, 82, 129, 141, 143, 146
Koob, Roger 17, 36, 37, 40, 81, 82, 130, 141, 146
Koplik, Jim 97, 120, 126, 127
Kravitz, Lenny 109

INDEX

Kugell, Marty 32, 41, 137

L

Laine, Denny 120
Lake Compounce 27, 37, 110, 124, 130, 141
Led Zeppelin 25, 79, 103
Leka, Paul 32, 113, 161, 164, 165, 166
Lennon, John 35
Levene, Ivor 20, 80, 85
Levitt Pavilion 35, 53, 93, 109
Lewis, Huey 175
Lewis, Jerry Lee 38
Lightfoot, Gordon 37, 87, 102
Little Richard 30, 34, 35, 76, 115, 123

M

Maggie Band 164, 166
Marble Collection, the 147
Marley, Bob & the Wailers 38
Matthews, Dave 120, 121
Max Creek, band 151
Mayer, John 115, 121, 122
McCartney, Linda 84, 128
McCartney, Paul 35, 80, 84, 100, 120, 159, 160
McNulty, Henry 21, 52, 102, 169
Meadows Music Theatre 27, 58, 79, 80, 85, 99, 104, 105, 111, 114, 117, 120, 121, 124, 151
Meat Loaf 85, 106, 115
MGMT, band 103, 104
Michael Bolton 68, 175

"Michael Row the Boat Ashore" 134
Midnite Movers, the 147
Miller, Cheri, Cheri Shack 66, 67, 68
Moby 111
Mohegan Sun 12, 27, 29, 42, 58, 79, 80, 85, 104, 105, 109, 115, 116, 117, 118, 121, 122, 124, 125, 151
Montowese House, music venue 69, 70, 71
Moore, Thurston 113, 114
Morissette, Alanis 117
Morrison, Jim 16, 19, 61, 100, 146
Murray the K 20, 46, 116
Music Explosion, the 38, 43, 44, 172

N

NAIF, band 69
"(Na Na Hey Hey) Kiss Him Goodbye" 161, 162, 163, 164, 165
Napi Browne, band 55, 62, 94, 113
Nelson, Ricky 42, 85
Nevins, Biggie, Connecticut Bandstand 131, 132, 143
New England band 27, 28, 29, 113, 120, 121, 141, 145
New Haven Arena 11, 16, 17, 18, 19, 20, 21, 22, 31, 35, 37, 57, 84, 88, 93, 99, 130, 145
New Haven Coliseum, the 15, 16, 18, 22, 23, 24, 26, 27, 29, 35, 79, 80, 104, 121
New Haven Green 35, 116

INDEX

New Haven Paramount Theatre 31, 37
No Doubt, band 27
"No Good to Cry" 60
NRBQ, the 50, 51, 52, 61, 91, 92, 93, 106
Nutmegs, the 17, 30, 31, 37, 38, 81
Nyro, Laura 12, 88
Nyro, Nyro 88

O

Oakdale Theatre 12, 35, 49, 53, 58, 61, 79, 80, 88, 97, 98, 99, 100, 101, 102, 103, 104, 105, 114, 117, 120, 121, 122, 124, 173
Ohlman, Christine 15, 61, 65, 91, 92, 94, 95, 96, 113, 171
"Only a Lonely Heart Sees" 98, 160
"Only Love Can Break a Heart" 42

P

Page, Jimmy 118
Parris, Fred 17, 31, 32, 139, 166, 173
Petty, Tom 27, 120
Philamonjaro, Phillip Solomonson 22, 24, 79, 86, 149, 150
Pinecrest Country Club 27, 85, 93
Pitney, Gene 30, 38, 40, 41, 42, 43, 44, 47, 48, 49, 73, 75, 117, 123, 137, 144
Plant, Robert 79
Playmates, the, group 73, 74
Potter, Jeff 60, 62, 67
Powder Ridge Festival, the 76

Premiers 17, 29, 30, 31, 36, 37, 40, 41, 81, 82, 129, 130, 141, 142, 143, 146
Presley, Elvis 16, 23, 24, 34, 83, 84, 167
Pulse, the 55, 61, 62, 65, 67, 69, 104, 113, 122
Pyramids, the 130, 140

Q

Quigley Stadium 37, 81, 82

R

Raitt, Bonnie 50, 51, 57, 58, 93, 103
Rascals, the 11, 12, 17, 21, 22, 49, 78, 98, 99, 115, 119, 145, 159, 160
Ready, Steady, Go, TV show 42
Reducers, the 48, 51, 96, 106
Richards, Keith 34, 108, 109, 153, 154
Ridgefield Playhouse, the 12, 110, 116, 125, 150
Robinson, Dick, WDRC DJ 84, 174
Rock 'n' Roll Hall of Fame 21, 24, 25, 27, 34, 35, 40, 42, 57, 79, 80, 84, 86, 88, 90, 95, 99, 102, 104, 108, 109, 115, 116, 117, 119, 120, 124, 144, 145, 150
Rolling Stones, the 20, 25, 34, 35, 42, 84, 90, 108, 109, 153
Ron and His Rattletones, group 130
Ronettes, the 40, 116, 171
Rosano, Paul 55, 62, 67, 113

Index

Rosenay, Charles 84, 127, 128, 173, 175
Ross, Diana 57, 124

S

Scarlets, the 30, 31, 32
Shaboo Inn, the 12, 15, 49, 50, 51, 54, 58, 93, 96, 99, 104, 111, 125
Shaboo Spirit, the 50, 51
Shaboo Stage, the 50, 51, 53
Shaboo, the 51
Shack, the 59, 60, 61, 62, 63, 93
Shags, the 21, 22, 48, 49, 61, 104, 111, 112, 139
Shea, Gary 27, 28, 29
Sia, Joe, famed photographer 56, 57
Simms Brothers, band 114
Simon, Paul 79, 120
Sinatra, Frank 15, 29, 123
Sly and the Family Stone 21, 82
Snoop Dog 120
Songwriters Hall of Fame 35, 88, 104, 115
South Michigan Avenue, the 59, 63, 83
Spears, Britney 105
Spector, Phil 42, 116
Spector, Ronnie 12, 40, 116, 119, 171
Springsteen, Bruce 85, 106, 120
Staples High School 12, 21, 75, 99, 118
Starr, Ringo 12, 99, 117, 124
Steam, band 161, 163, 164, 165, 166
Stefani, Gwen 27

Stewart, Rod 90
Sting 93, 104, 110, 151
Sultans, the 74, 75, 76
Supremes, the 57, 124
Swift, Taylor 121
Symbolix, the 21, 22, 67, 145
Syncron Recording Studios, Trod Nossel 62

T

Talking Heads, band 51, 106, 109
Toad's Place 15, 16, 27, 35, 50, 58, 84, 85, 88, 93, 96, 106, 107, 108, 109, 110, 111, 112, 113, 114, 115, 125, 149, 151
"To Be or Not to Be" 64
Tommy and The Rivieras 19
"Too Good to Be True" 134
Tork, Peter 53, 54
Toto, band 126
Tyler, Steven 52, 118

U

U2 27, 106
Upbeats, the 147

V

Valli, Frankie 145
Van Dykes, the 130, 139, 145
Vee, Bobby 42
Village Maid Band 54
Vocal Group Hall of Fame 31, 40, 99, 145

W

Who, the 26, 48, 102
Wildweeds, the 48, 50, 59, 60, 61,
    65, 67, 68, 91, 92, 93, 94, 95,
    96, 100, 101, 144
Wilson, Brian 102, 115, 116, 119,
    120, 123
Winter, Edgar 51, 103, 106, 125
Winter, Johnny 51, 106, 115, 118,
    119, 125, 126
Woodstock 37, 51, 56, 125, 149
Woolsey Hall 27, 54, 55, 56, 57, 58

Y

Yale Bowl, the 12, 15, 22, 78, 79,
    80
Yardbirds, the 86, 90, 118
Yesterday's Children, band 64
Young, Neil 84, 87, 88
Young Rascals, the 11, 21, 22, 99,
    145

Z

Zombies, the 119

ABOUT THE AUTHOR

Photo by Mary Ellen Blacker.

Tony Renzoni is the author of the well-received books *Connecticut Rock 'n' Roll: A History*, *Connecticut Softball Legend Joan Joyce* and *Connecticut Bootlegger Queen Nellie Green*.

His new book *Connecticut Music Venues: From the Coliseum to Shaboo* is the second in his series on rock 'n' roll in Connecticut.

Tony is a rock 'n' roll enthusiast. He was an avid collector of rock memorabilia for many years, amassing a record collection of over ten thousand vinyl records. One of his hobbies has been researching the rock 'n' roll music scene in Connecticut, as well as nationally.

Tony had a thirty-eight-year career with the federal government. As district manager in Connecticut's Fairfield County, he oversaw the operations of four field offices, serving over 100,000 beneficiaries. He wrote over one thousand weekly columns that were published in the *Connecticut Post* newspaper and on the paper's website. Tony was a recipient of more than forty awards, including his agency's highest honor award.

Tony Renzoni is a graduate of Sacred Heart University in Fairfield and is a lifelong resident of Connecticut.

Visit us at
www.historypress.com

v

www.ingramcontent.com/pod-product-compliance
Lightning Source LLC
Chambersburg PA
CBHW070357100426
42812CB00005B/1533